New Directions for
Teaching and Learning

Catherine M. Wehlburg
EDITOR-IN-CHIEF

From the Confucian Way to Collaborative Knowledge Co-Construction

Gertina J. van Schalkwyk
Rik Carl D'Amato

EDITORS

Number 142 • Summer 2015
Jossey-Bass
San Francisco

FROM THE CONFUCIAN WAY TO COLLABORATIVE KNOWLEDGE CO-CONSTRUCTION
Gertina J. van Schalkwyk, Rik Carl D'Amato (eds.)
New Directions for Teaching and Learning, no. 142
Catherine M. Wehlburg, Editor-in-Chief

Microfilm copies of issues and articles are available in 16 mm and 35 mm, as well as microfiche in 105 mm, through University Microfilms, Inc., 300 North Zeeb Road, Ann Arbor, MI 48106-1346.

NEW DIRECTIONS FOR TEACHING AND LEARNING (ISSN 0271-0633, electronic ISSN 1536-0768) is part of The Jossey-Bass Higher and Adult Education Series and is published quarterly by Wiley Subscription Services, Inc., A Wiley Company, at Jossey-Bass, One Montgomery Street, Suite 1200, San Francisco, CA 94104-4594. POSTMASTER: Send address changes to New Directions for Teaching and Learning, Jossey-Bass, One Montgomery Street, Suite 1200, San Francisco, CA 94104-4594.

New Directions for Teaching and Learning is indexed in CIJE: Current Index to Journals in Education (ERIC), Contents Pages in Education (T&F), Educational Research Abstracts Online (T&F), ERIC Database (Education Resources Information Center), Higher Education Abstracts (Claremont Graduate University), and SCOPUS (Elsevier).

INDIVIDUAL SUBSCRIPTION RATE (in USD): $89 per year US/Can/Mex, $113 rest of world; institutional subscription rate: $335 US, $375 Can/Mex, $409 rest of world. Single copy rate: $29. Electronic only–all regions: $89 individual, $335 institutional; Print & Electronic–US: $98 individual, $402 institutional; Print & Electronic–Can/Mex: $98 individual, $442 institutional; Print & Electronic–rest of world: $122 individual, $476 institutional.

Cover design: Wiley
Cover Images: © Lava 4 images | Shutterstock

EDITORIAL CORRESPONDENCE should be sent to the editor-in-chief, Catherine M. Wehlburg, c.wehlburg@tcu.edu.

www.josseybass.com

CONTENTS

FROM THE SERIES EDITOR

About This Publication

Since 1980, *New Directions for Teaching and Learning* (NDTL) has brought a unique blend of theory, research, and practice to leaders in postsecondary education. NDTL sourcebooks strive not only for solid substance but also for timeliness, compactness, and accessibility.

The series has four goals: to inform readers about current and future directions in teaching and learning in postsecondary education, to illuminate the context that shapes these new directions, to illustrate these new direction through examples from real settings, and to propose ways in which these new directions can be incorporated into still other settings.

This publication reflects the view that teaching deserves respect as a high form of scholarship. We believe that significant scholarship is conducted not only by researchers who report results of empirical investigations but also by practitioners who share disciplinary reflections about teaching. Contributors to NDTL approach questions of teaching and learning as seriously as they approach substantive questions in their own disciplines, and they deal not only with pedagogical issues but also with the intellectual and social context in which these issues arise. Authors deal on the one hand with theory and research and on the other with practice, and they translate from research and theory to practice and back again.

About This Volume

The purpose of this first volume of a two-part series is to assist lecturers, educators, and teachers in Asian contexts in choreographing collaborative teaching and learning experiences with adult learners in higher education settings. For instructors coming from more Western-oriented educational experiences and where the teacher–student relationship is more egalitarian and learning involves active participation in argumentation and rhetoric, the shift toward collaborative teaching and learning may not be that big. Instructors often are familiar with challenging old ideas and exploring new ways of solving problems not yet defined. However, to qualify as an effective teacher of collaborative knowledge co-construction, one is required to do more than lecture and direct the line of thinking through demonstration in the classroom. The instructor should not teach but rather facilitate learning by stimulating creativity, self-learning, collaboration, and critical thinking.

Catherine M. Wehlburg
Editor-in-Chief

PROLOGUE

Dedications

To my family and friends in Asia and elsewhere, and the numerous students I have met over the years: Thank you for your inspiration, support, and collaboration choreographing this book. I dedicate this book as a tribute to all of you!

—Gertina J. van Schalkwyk

To Marcia, Gertina, Katherine, Bo, Liz, Mandy, Angelina, Yuanyuan, and my numerous friends in Macao SAR, China: I could not have made it without your continuous support and love. You taught me so much and I am grateful!

—Rik Carl D'Amato

Prologue

In dance literature, the term "choreography" refers to the art of designing, planning, and arranging sequences of movements, patterns, and actions leading up to an event. Performers combine a range of choreographic techniques and improvisation to create meaning through their active engagement with the directives of the choreographer. Whereas planned choreography dictates motion and form in detail, improvisation offers latitude for personal interpretation, all with the aim of achieving a shared goal or vision. Although the concept of choreography is mostly used to refer to fields such as dance, gymnastics, ice skating, and other dance compositions, it can also be used as metaphor for the planning and arrangement of actions leading up to an event in other settings. In an educational setting, the instructor can act as a choreographer who has a vision or objective for the course he or she is teaching and arranges a series of actions, interactions, and co-actions that will lead to effective learning. Choreographing in this context, then, is a metaphor referring to the rhythmic dance evolving between instructor and learner in the educational setting within higher education.

New Directions for Teaching and Learning, no. 142, Summer 2015 © 2015 Wiley Periodicals, Inc.
Published online in Wiley Online Library (wileyonlinelibrary.com) • DOI: 10.1002/tl.20126

The choreographer or director guides the actors on the stage through their paces, often training them in specific skills with the goal of staging a successful performance. Similarly, the instructor in a higher education setting facilitates the collaborative actions and co-actions aimed at achieving the envisioned outcomes of learning. Merely asking students to work together as a team or assigning a group task without careful planning and understanding of the intricate dynamics underlying collaborative teaching and learning will not succeed. The instructor needs to plan and guide students through various challenges and uncertainties of individual and group work in order for them to develop the skills necessary for learning to be meaningful. Choreographing an outcomes-based collaborative teaching and learning (OBCTL) environment aims to facilitate the internalization of skills and attitudes where students can appreciate their personal knowledge and develop confidence in themselves. The students, among themselves and with the instructor, engage in different dances as they collaboratively reflect on existing knowledge systems, explore different perspectives, and move, for example, from just learning and memorizing theoretical constructs, to thinking about the influence of personal experience and to interpreting observations in accordance with relevant theory or empirical work.

Collaborative teaching and learning for the co-construction of new meanings in an academic environment is no easy task. It is particularly challenging when the culture of teaching and learning in Asian educational systems is embedded in the Confucian heritage culture, which defines the positioning of instructor and student in an almost nonnegotiable power hierarchy. The rules of engagement and of interpretation and cognitive processes are somehow different, and students often find it difficult to express their views in the language of tuition (e.g., English), with which they may not feel competent conversing. Sharing in the process of knowledge construction seems almost a violation of their existing "realities" and is a foreign concept for many Asian students in a higher education setting.

The chapters in this volume provide instructors coming from a more Western-oriented educational experience, where the teacher–student relationship is more egalitarian and learning involves active participation in argumentation and rhetoric, with guidelines for doing OBCTL in a higher education setting. As the choreographer, the instructor should not teach but rather facilitate learning by stimulating creativity, self-learning, and critical thinking. Knowledge of current instructional design strategies and the OBCTL approach proposed in this text also help instructors to find new ways of motivating and engaging Asian students in collaborative efforts and deep learning. The authors in this volume review learning in the Confucian way and provide insight into the unique learning motivation of contemporary students in Confucian heritage cultures, explaining the interrelationship between outcomes-based education and collaborative teaching and learning. They provide practical guidelines for planning a course that integrates the key elements of OBCTL and for adapting instructional design and lesson planning to fit the unique characteristics of Asian students. From the design and planning phase to choreographing in-class and out-of-class performances, the authors present a variety of tried and tested strategies and projects of learning, authentic assessment, and blended learning for motivating and engaging Asian students in learning outcomes with local and global relevance. We hope you will join us in helping Confucian heritage culture students understand and prosper using a collaborative model of teaching and learning.

Gertina J. van Schalkwyk
Rik Carl D'Amato
Editors

GERTINA J. VAN SCHALKWYK *is an associate professor of psychology and head of the Department of Psychology, and former coordinator for professional development in the Centre for Teaching and Learning Enhancement at the University of Macau, China.*

RIK CARL D'AMATO *is a professor of psychology on the faculty of the Chicago School of Professional Psychology, and former director of the Centre for Teaching and Learning Enhancement at the University of Macau, China.*

1

In this chapter, the focus is on understanding the unique learning motivations shared by contemporary students in Confucian heritage cultures.

Learning the Confucian Way

Tieyuan Guo

Confucius was a great philosopher and educator in ancient China. His followers recorded his thoughts and philosophy in *The Analects*. Confucian philosophy developed around 551 to 479 BC, and included his ideas on learning and education. His philosophy has had a fundamental influence on contemporary people all over Asia (including Mainland China, Hong Kong, Macao, Taiwan, Japan, Korea, and Southeast Asia). Contemporary students in Confucian heritage culture (CHC) contexts share some similar motivations, strategies, and beliefs about learning. Understanding of those learning motivations can help non-Asian instructors to deliver their teaching in a way that fits the cultural context and thus teach more effectively. Knowing about the strategies and beliefs can help instructors understand the advantages and shortcomings of the Confucian way of learning and recognize how to adjust their teaching strategies to meet the needs of students. Furthermore, an awareness of the common misunderstandings about Asian students' learning will prevent instructors from making wrong or unnecessary demands on the students. Finally, this chapter addresses some signs that indicate active and deep learning and other signs that indicate passive and surface learning in CHC contexts; understanding these signs can help instructors from making wrong judgments about students' learning.

Learning Motivations in Confucian Heritage Culture Contexts

This chapter explores the historical objectives of education in Asian countries where a typical Confucian approach and input-driven teaching and learning style is evident. To begin, the chapter first discusses the learning motivations shared by many contemporary students in Confucian heritage culture (CHC) contexts. Then the focus is on the methods of and beliefs about learning emphasized in Asian countries and regions. These methods and beliefs include the emphasis on effort and persistence in learning, the

NEW DIRECTIONS FOR TEACHING AND LEARNING, no. 142, Summer 2015 © 2015 Wiley Periodicals, Inc.
Published online in Wiley Online Library (wileyonlinelibrary.com) • DOI: 10.1002/tl.20127

active learning strategies in the Confucian tradition, humbleness and respect for authority figures, and memorization and deep learning.

Personal Moral Cultivation.   Confucius and his followers believed that the primary goal of learning was to achieve behavioral reform and make the learner become a moral person. The concept of *ren* is fundamental in Confucius's teaching, and refers to a "lifelong striving for any human being to become the most genuine, sincere, and humane person he or she can become" (Li 2003, 146). Confucius was most concerned that virtues were not cultivated and that wrong acts were not corrected (Legge 2005). In the *Great Learning*, one of the *Four Books*, Confucius's followers argued that in order to govern a state properly, one needed to improve oneself in virtue through learning (Legge 2005). A person's virtue is the key for proper behavior in all respects. Overall, Confucius's teaching was full of moral teaching.

The idea of moral learning has had great influence on contemporary students in countries with CHC. Students in CHC contexts consider prolonged discourse on social norms, morality, and moral constraints on behavior in school settings more acceptable than do those in Western cultures (Bellah et al. 1985; Li 1996; Tweed and Lehman 2002). Li (2002) found that Chinese college students were more likely to consider learning as fulfilling a need to perfect oneself instead of understanding the world. The students almost unanimously (93 percent) considered that learning had something to do with moral development. In another study, Li (2004) investigated American and Chinese children's construction of the learning process and found that Chinese children were more likely to consider learning to be a process of cultivating personal virtue. Thus, it seems that Chinese students learn for different reasons.

Contributing to Society.   In Confucian tradition, educated people have social and moral responsibilities to contribute to society after they had achieved behavioral reform and had become moral through learning (Li 2003). Educated people should become government servants and serve the nation, because learning had prepared them for successful government services and for achieving any mission that might come to them (*The Analects: Book 13, Chapter 5*). In order to be competent as a government servant, Confucius told his students that they needed to rectify themselves and become a model for the people under their rule through learning (*The Analects: Book 13, Chapter 13*). Confucius saw learning and serving the government as closely associated. Tsze-hsia, one of Confucius's students, said that the government officer, having discharged all his duties, should devote his or her leisure time to learning. Meanwhile, students who excel in study should become government officers (*The Analects: Book 19, Chapter 13*). Indeed, in Chinese history, an important criterion for selecting government servant candidates is good education. Since the Sui dynasty (AD 581–618), the imperial examination system, known as *keju*, had been used to select government servant candidates. With minor alterations, this examination was used in each subsequent dynasty until it was abolished in 1905. Throughout the almost 1,500 years of its existence, *keju* assisted the selection of government officials (Carless 2011).

Personal Utilitarian Orientation.   Although Confucius rarely if at all considered the personal utilitarian purpose of learning, the imperial examination system inevitably linked the two (Li 2003). In the *keju* system, studying the required subjects and passing the examinations became the major track for upward social mobility (Cheng 1998). Nonetheless, some researchers argue that, compared with the learning motivations among students in Western countries, students in Confucian heritage cultures tend to be more pragmatic in learning (Lee 1996; Tweed and Lehman 2002). That is, learning is not merely for the sake of learning itself but for obtaining external rewards. Tweed and Lehman (2002, 92) used the term "pragmatic learning" to characterize this tendency. Learning is considered a means to an end (Carless 2011; Lee 1996; Tweed and Lehman 2002) and can lose its meaning if it does not provide the learner and the society with desirable pragmatic outcomes. The Chinese idiom, "There are golden houses and beautiful women in books," reflects the seeking of external rewards, such as fame, wealth, and social status in learning (Lee 1996).

Given the emphasis of a pragmatic outcome in Confucian heritage cultures, it is not surprising to learn that learners in Asian contexts may show more curiosity toward practical issues rather than theoretical issues. In one of their studies, Spina and Ji (2011) presented Chinese and Canadian college students with two lectures on physics: One lecture was on the theoretical implications of a physics finding, and the other was on the practical use of the same finding. The Chinese students reported that they were more likely to attend the lecture on practical issues than did the Canadian students. Thus, in order to motivate the learners in an Asian context, it is a good idea to point out some practical outcomes of the learning contents. For example, one such pragmatic outcome could be future career development.

In contemporary CHC, students pay close attention to the practical implications of education. Compared with Western students, students in CHC contexts generally believe that education should provide them with prestigious jobs and high social status. For example, in one study, Volet (2001) compared Australian students and Singaporean/Malay Chinese students on extrinsic goal orientations in learning and found that Chinese students were more motivated by pragmatic outcomes of education, such as getting a good job after graduation, satisfying the families' expectations, and obtaining social respect.

One consequence of the pragmatic learning motivation is examination-oriented learning and teaching. That is, students emphasize the importance of examinations and achievements because passing the examinations and having high grades are the keys to desirable outcomes (Carless

2011). Students with this orientation tend to spend more time preparing for examinations. As a result, students in CHC contexts are often good test takers. Compared to Western students, they generally have more successful achievements in international tests, such as the Program for International Assessment (PISA) (Carless 2011; Na 2010). The PISA 2009 assessed students' abilities in reading, mathematics, and science in 65 countries and regions. According to the results, four Confucian countries and regions—Mainland China, Singapore, Hong Kong, and Korea—were the top four highest achievers in mathematics. For reading and science, four out of the top five highest-achievement countries and regions were CHC contexts (Organisation of Economic Cooperation and Development 2009).

The emphasis on pragmatic outcomes in learning in CHC does not imply that students in those cultures are less intrinsically motivated. That is, the seeking of external rewards through learning among the Asian students does not preclude them from being intrinsically interested in learning itself. Indeed, researchers have suggested that the intrinsic motivation tends to co-occur with extrinsic motivation in CHC contexts (Lee 1996; Salili, Chiu, and Lai 2001; Tweed and Lehman 2002). Students who see learning as a means to obtain desirable external outcomes are more motivated to mastering knowledge. They integrate aspirations of obtaining external rewards through education with the intrinsic motivation of personal growth. Although it may seem foreign to non-Asian instructors, it may be very effective in motivating students in CHC contexts by pointing out the potential pragmatic outcomes of successful learning.

Valuing of Education.   Education is highly valued in the Confucian tradition. The opening sentence of Confucius's *Analects* (*Book 1, Chapter 1*) talks about the joy of constant learning (Legge 2005). In fact, that discussion about learning and education pervades the whole book of *The Analects* (Legge 2005). In a CHC, the key to personal improvement is education. Through education, a person can transform him- or herself and become a moral and able person, or *junzi*. Education is also important for social harmony and development because the government needs educated people to govern the nation efficiently (Lee 1996).

Given the significance of education in the Confucian tradition, contemporary students in CHC contexts are highly motivated to learn. They have high achievement goals and are generally willing to invest a lot of time in learning. Meanwhile, parents have high educational expectations for their children because they regard education as the main track of upward social mobility (Cheng 1997), and students in Confucian heritage cultures internalize these expectations (Carless 2011). Students become highly motivated in academics because their success in schools can earn respect and fame for their family, which is highly valued in Confucian societies. This might be another reason why students in CHC contexts outperform Western students on many international comparison tests, as previously mentioned.

Beliefs and Strategies of Learning

Confucius and his followers placed strong emphasis on the significance of persistence and hard work in learning (Carless 2011; Li 2003; Tweed and Lehman 2002). Confucius did not refuse to teach anyone who wanted to learn (*Analects, Book 7, Chapter 7*), except those who were not eager to work hard in learning (*Analects, Book 7, Chapter 8*) (Legge 2005). Xunzi, another Confucian scholar in ancient China, also emphasized persistence and effort in learning and argued, "If you start carving but give up, you cannot cut even a rotting piece of wood in two. Yet, if you carve away and never give up, even metal and stone can be engraved" (Knoblock 1988, 138).

Persistent and Effortful Learning. Research supports the notion that CHC emphasizes persistence and effort in learning. Chinese parents, teachers, and students firmly believe in the power of effort in improving academic performance and contributing to success (Ji 2008; Ji, Guo, Zhang, and Messervey 2009; Stevenson and Lee 1996; Stevenson and Stigler 1992). Chinese students tend to attribute academic success to hard work (Hau and Salili 1991) rather than to some internal attribute or quality. They also devote a lot of effort to the process of learning. Rosenthal and Feldman (1991) compared Chinese immigrant students and their Western peers in Australia and the United States with regard to the amount of effort they put in study. Chinese students reported putting much more effort into school than did their Western peers.

Research also suggests that people who believe in the power of effort tend to hold implicit incremental theories (Dweck, Chiu, and Hong 1995; Hong et al. 1999). Incremental theorists believe that traits, intelligence, and ability are malleable, and thus changeable, and that academic success comes from efforts and practices (Dweck 1999; Dweck and Leggett 1988). In contrast, those who hold entity theories believe that traits, intelligence, and ability are fixed and cannot be changed. As a result, entity theorists are more likely attribute academic success to stable, unchangeable intelligence and ability rather than effort. Norenzayan, Choi, and Nisbett (2002) suggested that East Asians are more likely to hold incremental theories than Westerners.

Furthermore, incremental theorists and entity theorists may respond differently when encountering difficulties and failures in learning. Entity theorists may attribute the difficulties and failures to low intelligence and ability, which are fixed and unchangeable. As a result, they may easily give up after failure. In contrast, incremental theorists see the difficulties and failures as the results of insufficient effort. By putting in more effort and being persistent, learners can overcome the difficulties and obtain success (Ji 2008; Tweed and Lehman 2002). Compared with entity theorists, incremental theorists tend to persevere longer and perform better after failure (Levy and Dweck 1998). Persistence and effort pay off in academic achievements. Blackwell, Trzesniewski, and Dweck (2007) found that beliefs in incremental theory predicted an upward trajectory of grades for junior high school students over a two-year period of time, while beliefs in entity theory predicted a flat trajectory.

In CHC contexts, instructors and parents expect persistence and effort from learners when they encounter difficulties and failures in learning. Difficulties and failures can lead to future success because they provide the opportunity for learners to exercise and improve themselves. Mencius (1979, VIB.15:261) expressed this idea, saying that "when [heaven] is about to place a great burden on a man, [it] always first tests his resolution, exhausts his frame and makes him suffer starvation and hardship, frustrates his efforts so as to shake him from his mental lassitude, toughen his nature and make good his deficiencies. As a rule, a man can mend his ways only after he has made mistakes."

Heine and colleagues (2001) found that students in CHC contexts persisted longer after failure than did Western students. In one study, they assigned either an easy task or a difficult task to Canadian and Japanese college students. Both groups received success feedback for the easy task and failure feedback for the difficult task. After receiving the feedback, the students had the opportunity to continue working on a similar task of their own choice. The researchers found that Japanese students spent much longer on the similar task than did their Canadian counterparts in the difficulty-failure condition, suggesting that Japanese students persisted longer after failure.

Active Learning in Confucian Heritage Culture Contexts.   An instructor from United States, who was teaching at a Chinese university, once complained that the Chinese students in his classes seemed very passive. To the American instructor, the Chinese students seemed to be extremely quiet in the classroom—they rarely raised any questions, were not active in class activities, and were reluctant to express their own ideas. Other Western-trained instructors made similar observations. These observations may suggest that students from Confucian heritage cultures are passive in learning. However, as Grimshaw (2007) points out, this might be a misperception. The failure to ask questions and to talk does not imply that students from CHC contexts are passive in learning. Actually, the Chinese students in the American instructor's classes might have engaged in active learning processes.

Confucius did not put much value on talking, as can be seen in his sayings "be careful with speech" (*The Analects, Book 1, Chapter 14*) and "The man of perfect virtue is cautious and slow in speech" (*The Analects, Book 12, Chapter 3*) (Legge 2005). In his teachings, Confucius considered being silent an effective way of learning (*The Analects, Book 7, Chapter 2*) (Legge 2005). In Confucian tradition, being silent may indicate reflection, cognitive involvement, and being active in deep thinking. In contrast, Western cultures consider talking as closely related to thinking. Throughout the history of Confucian teaching, the connection between talking and thinking is rarely discussed. Instead, people in CHC contexts tend to assume that silence and introspection imply high levels of thinking and learning, such as realizing the "supreme truth" through meditation in Taoism (Robinet 1993). Kim (2002) investigated the effects of talking on thinking. In one experiment, Asian Americans and European Americans talked aloud about their thinking processes while solving reasoning problems in an intelligence test. The results showed that talking impaired the performance for the Asian Americans but not the European Americans. Instead of passivity, the relative silence in the classroom in Confucian heritage cultures may therefore actually indicate that students are active in thinking and reflection and thus are actively involved in learning.

Furthermore, collectivist cultural values do not encourage the individual to initiate questions (Hofstede and Hofstede 2005). Compared to individualist cultures where the ties between individuals are loose, in collectivist cultures, people are integrated into strong, cohesive groups (Hofstede 2001). Collectivism prevails in CHC contexts, such as in Mainland China, Hong Kong, Japan, Korea, Singapore, and elsewhere. This concept is expressed by the old Japanese proverb, "The nail that stands out gets pounded down." In collectivist cultures, people avoid standing out from their groups because it may result in conflict and jeopardize group harmony (Tafarodi, Marshall, and Katsura 2004). Thus, in a collectivist classroom, students are reluctant to speak up without the sanction of the group or invitation from the teacher (Carless 2011). Students may be too shy or worry about losing face in front of the class if the questions they initiate or the talk they give are inappropriate or incorrect. The quiet classroom may be just an outcome of the cultural norm instead of the result of passivity in learning.

Meanwhile, the large power distance in CHC contexts also discourages students from openly questioning their teachers (Carless 2011). Power distance, another cultural dimension proposed by Hofstede (2001), refers to the extent to which the less powerful members accept and expect the unequal distribution of power. Compared to Western cultures, CHC contexts tend to have high power distance (Hofstede 2001). Students in high-power-distance cultures expect the teacher to enforce strict order over the classroom. They see the teachers and the textbooks as highly authoritative sources of knowledge that should not be questioned (Carless 2011; Pratt, Kelly, and Wong 1999). Reluctance to ask challenging questions of the teacher and not speaking up unless invited by the teacher are therefore signs of respect for the authority of the teacher (Tweed and Lehman 2002). A quest for humility further adds to students' reluctance to question the teacher and speak out in the classroom. Confucius regarded humility as a virtue, and students in CHC contexts are reluctant to speak up because they believe that humility ensures better learning (Li 2003).

The teachings of Confucius put strong emphasis on the acquisition of knowledge through attentiveness (Tweed and Lehman 2002). Students listen to lectures attentively and question only after they fully understand what has been taught (Li 2003). Pratt et al. (1999) also suggested that both teachers and students construe learning in Confucian heritage cultures as a sequential four-stage process: (1) memorizing and mastering the basics, (2) understanding, (3) applying the knowledge to problems and situations, and (4) questioning or critical analyzing. Students should first commit the foundational knowledge and basics to memory. In the process of repetition and memorization, students should increase their attention to the content details and thus deepen their understanding of the learning materials. Thus, memorization is purposeful and appropriate for developing understanding. Only after memorizing and appropriately understanding the foundational knowledge should students apply learning to problems and situations. Memorization guarantees that the knowledge is available when needed, and appropriate and deep understanding ensures that the knowledge applied properly to problems and situations. Questioning and higher-level critical learning are expected only at the last stage of learning, usually after encountering new problems or new situations.

Because students in CHC contexts tend to see the teacher and the texts as highly authoritative sources of knowledge, they are more likely to operate in a recipient mode in the process of learning rather than challenging and questioning. They may be busy in engaging in the first three stages and postpone their questions to a later time (i.e., after the class time). In the Confucian tradition, active learning is reflected more in cognitive involvement, lesson preparation, reflection and review, thinking, and memorization rather than being active in talking and questioning (Cortazzi and Jin 1996). One learning strategy in Confucian teaching was that the review and reflection of old knowledge contributed to the process of learning knew knowledge (*The Analects, Book 2, Chapter 11*) (Legge 2005). Thus, teachers should neither consider the silence in the classroom as evidence of passive learning nor consider active talking and questioning in the classroom as the sign of active engagement in learning (Grimshaw 2007).

Although silence in the classroom is not solid evidence for passivity in CHC contexts, teachers should be aware that passivity and inattention could occur in quiet classrooms. In CHC contexts, inattention and passivity in learning are possible. Grimshaw (2007) argues that withdrawal of attention (e.g., sleeping, reading other materials in the class, using mobile devices, etc.) and being silent are also forms of protest by Chinese students when the teacher presents the lecture poorly or when students see the contents of learning as unimportant and impractical. In such cases, the learning atmosphere of the classroom is gloomy and uninviting of learning. Therefore, the instructor should take responsibility to ensure that passivity and inattention do not occur in her or his class.

In order to make sure that students pay attention in the class and learn actively, an instructor should regularly check for other signs of active learning in the classroom, such as lesson preparation or content review. In addition, teachers should try to be available to the students outside of the classroom, such as during the breaks between classes and after class and by setting up office hours or mechanisms through which students can contact them. Students would be more likely to approach teachers privately to discuss the learning materials and ask questions if they have actively engaged in learning, because they may feel more comfortable to talk in such informal ways. If teachers are available outside of the classroom and no student comes to discuss any questions, the teachers should be very aware that students are exhibiting passivity and inattention to the learning context.

Memorization in Confucian Heritage Culture Contexts

As discussed previously, the Confucian tradition strongly emphasized the acquisition of knowledge. In Confucian teaching, memorizing the classics is essential in developing virtues for the learners (Carless 2011). Students in CHC contexts see memorizing knowledge as the first stage of learning (Pratt et al. 1999; Tweed and Lehman 2002), and they widely use memorization in learning. Nonetheless, Westerners tend to perceive this emphasis of memorizing in CHC as a sign of surface-level learning (Biggs 1996; Tweed and Lehman 2002). According to Marton and Saljo (1976), surface-level learning happens when students try to memorize the materials by rote and repetition, without trying to understand the meaning. Contrary to surface learning, deep-level learning implies that students try to understand the meaning of the material rather than merely memorizing it. The emphasis on memorizing does not necessarily imply surface-level learning in CHC contexts (Carless 2011). Biggs (1996) distinguishes two types of learning strategies for memorization: rote learning and repetitive learning. In rote learning, students try to memorize the information through a mechanically repetitive manner without trying to understand the meaning. In contrast, in repetitive learning, although learners also try to form accurate memories through rehearsing the information, they try to understand the meaning from the learned material through the rehearsal.

In CHC contexts, memorization closely connects with understanding through repetitive learning. Memorization is a pathway to understanding and to the discovery of deep meanings of the learned materials. At the same time, understanding complements the memorization of the learning materials (Marton, Dall'Alba, and Kun 1996). As mentioned earlier, in the process of rehearsing the information, learners increase their attention to the information and consequently deepen their understanding and discover new meanings (Pratt et al. 1999). Thus, the emphasis on memorization in CHC contexts may actually reflect a deep approach to learning, which is aimed at a better understanding of the subject.

Students in CHC contexts who prefer to keep silent in the classroom, are reluctant to question others and express their own ideas, and are not very active in class activities often engage in memorizing the knowledge. These signs do not necessarily indicate passive and surface learning. In contrast, active and deep learning may take place. However, how can a teacher know

Table 1.1. Signs Indicating Active and Deep Learning versus Passive and Surface Learning

Signs	Active and Deep Learning	Passive and Surface Learning
Attentiveness	Students' eyes follow the teacher when the teacher moves around in the classroom or focus on the content presented. Students have eye contact with the teacher.	Students do not look at the teacher and/or the content presented. Beware if students avoid any eye contact.
	Students sit close to the teacher, preferring the first few rows of seats.	Students sit at the back of the classroom and leave the first few rows empty.
	Students take notes, write down their own thoughts and questions, even though they may not express their thoughts or raise the questions.	Students rarely write down anything.
	Students attend to the lecture and are able to express their understanding when invited.	Students pay attention to other unrelated things, such as reading unrelated books, messaging, dozing, and chatting.
Persistence	Students persist under failure, engage in discussions with other students for difficult questions, and/or come to the teacher for help during class breaks.	Students give up easily and avoid seeking help from the teacher.
Preparation	Students read the text before coming to the classroom and prepare necessary material for each week of class.	Students make no preparations and are not sure what the topic for each week of class is.
Reflection and review	Students spend time and effort reviewing the learning materials.	Students put away the learned contents and never review them until the examination.
Memorization	Students try to memorize the foundational knowledge and are able to talk about the meaning of the knowledge when invited.	Students do not memorize and/or have no understanding of the foundational knowledge.
Understanding and application	Students are interested in applying the learned knowledge to problems and situations.	Students are not interested in thinking about the learned knowledge outside of the classroom and rarely think about how to apply the knowledge.
Class attendance and participation	Students attend the class regularly, are rarely late or leave early, and are busy in class with relevant activities.	Students miss classes often, are late or leave early for no reason, and engage in unrelated activities.

if active and deep learning is actually taking place in the classroom? This is an important question, yet it is difficult to answer because no single sign or a small group of signs can clearly tell us which kind of learning is taking place. One rule in answering this question is that active and deep learning are more likely to take place when there are signs indicating that students invest a lot of time and effort in learning, devote attention to the learning, show interests in the lesson content, and try to understand and apply the learned knowledge. Table 1.1 summarizes some of these signs. By careful attention to students' behavior inside and outside of the classroom, instructors can develop their own set of signifiers to identify active and deep learning based on their own teaching experiences.

Conclusion

In order to achieve effective teaching in CHC contexts, rather than accepting various stereotypes they may have about the students, non-Asian instructors need to develop an understanding of the CHC context and the unique learning motivations, learning strategies and beliefs, and behavior of students. This chapter argued that students in CHC contexts value learning very much. Through learning, students expect to be able to become better people (i.e., personal moral cultivation and personal utility) and achieve a better world (i.e., contribute to society). In order to achieve these goals, students in CHC contexts generally believe in persistence and effort. Although they might remain quiet in the classroom and are reluctant to question teachers and express their own ideas, they could be engaging in active learning in the classroom. They may be busy trying to gain the knowledge and full understanding before questioning others or expressing their own thoughts.

Furthermore, memorization of foundational knowledge is an important way for students in CHC contexts to deepen their understanding. Teachers need to identify the signs indicating that learning is actually taking place in their classrooms and to distinguish between deep learning and surface learning. Students in CHC contexts outperform students in Western countries in many tests and examinations. Yet they postpone critical thinking and questioning and may often ignore the importance of critical thinking. Teachers familiar with the Western way of teaching can be at an advantage in improving the critical thinking skills of students and achieving better teaching outcomes by combining the Confucian way of teaching with Western teaching and learning. Instructors should encourage critical thinking in the classroom while adjusting teaching strategies to meet the needs of students. They should also accept that difference does not mean inferior—it should be respected while cultivating higher-order learning.

References

Bellah, R. N., R. Madsen, W. M. Sullivan, A. Swidler, and S. M. Tipton. 1985. *Habits of the Heart: Individualism and Commitment in American Life.* New York, NY: Harper and Row.

Biggs, J. 1996. "Western Misperceptions of the Confucian-Heritage Learning Culture." In *The Chinese Learner: Cultural, Psychological, and Contextual Influences,* edited by D. A. Watkins and J. B. Biggs, 45–68. Hong Kong, China: Comparative Education Research Centre and Australian Council for Educational Research.

Blackwell, L. S., K. H. Trzesniewski, and C. S. Dweck. 2007. "Implicit Theories of Intelligence Predict Achievement across an Adolescent Transition: A Longitudinal Study and an Intervention." *Child Development* 78: 246–263.

Carless, D. 2011. *From Testing to Productive Student Learning: Implementing Formative Assessment in Confucian Heritage Settings.* New York, NY: Taylor and Francis Group.

Cheng, K. M. 1997. "The Education System." In *Schooling in Hong Kong: Organisation, Teaching, and Social Context,* edited by G. Postiglione and W. O. Lee, 25–42. Hong Kong, China: Hong Kong University Press.

Cheng, K. M. 1998. "Can Education Values Be Borrowed? Looking into Cultural Differences." *Peabody Journal of Education* 73: 11–30.

Cortazzi, M., and L. Jin. 1996. "State of the Art Article: English Teaching and Learning in China." *Language Teaching* 29: 61–80.

Dweck, C. S. 1999. *Self-Theories: Their Role in Motivation, Personality, and Development.* Philadelphia, PA: Psychology Press.

Dweck, C. S., C. Chiu, and Y. Hong. 1995. "Implicit Theories and Their Role in Judgments and Reactions: A World from Two Perspectives." *Psychological Inquiry* 6: 267–285.

Dweck, C. S., and E. L. Leggett. 1988. "A Social-Cognitive Approach to Motivation and Personality." *Psychological Review* 95: 256–273.

Grimshaw, T. 2007. "Problematizing the Construct of 'the Chinese Learner': Insights from Ethnographic Research." *Educational Studies* 33: 299–311.

Hau, K. T., and F. Salili. 1991. "Structure and Semantic Differential Placement of Specific Causes: Academic Causal Attributions by Chinese Students in Hong Kong." *International Journal of Psychology* 26: 175–193.

Heine, S. J., S. Kitayama, D. R. Lehman, T. Takata, E. Ide, C. Leung, and H. Matsumoto. 2001. "Divergent Consequences of Success and Failure in Japan and North America: An Investigation of Self-Improving Motivations and Malleable Selves." *Journal of Personality and Social Psychology* 81: 599–615.

Hofstede, G. H. 2001. *Culture's Consequences: Comparing Values, Behaviors, Institutions, and Organizing across Nations.* Thousand Oaks, CA: Sage.

Hofstede, G. H., and G. J. Hofstede. 2005. *Cultures and Organizations: Software of the Mind,* 2nd ed. London, UK: McGraw-Hill.

Hong, Y. Y., C. Y. Chiu, C. S. Dweck, D. Lin, and W. Wan. 1999. "Implicit Theories, Attributions, and Coping: A Meaning System Approach." *Journal of Personality and Social Psychology* 77: 588–599.

Ji, L. J. 2008. "The Leopard Cannot Change His Spots, or Can He? Culture and the Development of Lay Theories of Change." *Personality and Social Psychology Bulletin* 34: 613–622.

Ji, L. J., T. Guo, Z. Zhang, and D. Messervey. 2009. "Looking into the Past: Cultural Differences in Perception and Representation of Past Information." *Journal of Personality and Social Psychology* 96: 761–769.

Kim, H. S. 2002. "We Talk, Therefore We Think? A Cultural Analysis of the Effect of Talking on Thinking." *Journal of Personality and Social Psychology* 83: 828–842.

Knoblock, J. 1988. *Xunzi: A Translation and Study of the Complete Works.* Stanford, CA: Stanford University Press.

Lee, W. O. 1996. "The Cultural Context for Chinese Learners: Conceptions of Learning in the Confucian Tradition. In *The Chinese Learner: Cultural, Psychological, and Contextual Influences*, edited by D. A. Watkins and J. B. Biggs, 45–68. Hong Kong, China: Comparative Education Research Centre and Australian Council for Educational Research.

Legge, J. 2005. *The Chinese Classics with a Translation, Critical and Exegetical Notes, Prolegomena, and Copious Indexes, Volume 1*, 2nd ed. London, UK: Oxford University Press.

Levy, S. R., and C. S. Dweck. 1998. "Trait- versus Process-Focused Social Judgment." *Social Cognition* 16: 151–172.

Li, J. 2002. "A Cultural Model of Learning: Chinese "Heart and Mind for Wanting to Learn." *Journal of Cross-Cultural Psychology* 33: 248–269.

Li, J. 2003. "The Core of Confucian Learning." *American Psychologist* 58: 146–147.

Li, J. 2004. "Learning as a Task or Virtue: U.S. and Chinese Preschoolers Explain Learning." *Development Psychology* 40: 595–605.

Li, X. 1996. *Good Writing in Cross-Cultural Context*. Albany: State University of New York Press.

Marton, F., G. Dall'Alba, and T. L. Kun. 1996. "Memorizing and Understanding: The Keys to the Paradox? In *The Chinese Learner: Cultural, Psychological, and Contextual Influences*, edited by D. A. Watkins and J. B. Biggs, 69–84. Hong Kong, China: Comparative Education Research Centre and Australian Council for Educational Research.

Marton, F., and R. Saljo. 1976. "On Qualitative Differences in Learning: 1. Outcome and Process." *British Journal of Educational Psychology* 46: 4–11.

Mencius. 1979. *Mencius*, translated by D. C. Lau. Hong Kong, China: The Chinese University Press.

Na, R. 2010. "Examining the Role of Age, Sex, and Cultural Background in the Motives in Educational Settings." *Journal of Language and Literature* 5: 168–170.

Norenzayan, A., I. Choi, and R. E. Nisbett. 2002. "Cultural Similarities and Differences in Social Inference: Evidence from Behavioral Predictions and Lay Theories of Behavior." *Personality and Social Psychology Bulletin* 28: 109–120.

Organisation of Economic Cooperation and Development. 2009. *PISA 2009 Scores and Rankings by Country/Economy*. http://www.oecd.org/pisa/46643496.pdf.

Pratt, D. D., M. Kelly, and W. S. S. Wong. 1999. "Chinese Conceptions of 'Effective Teaching' in Hong Kong: Towards Culturally Sensitive Evaluation of Teaching." *International Journal of Lifelong Education* 18: 241–258.

Robinet, I. 1993. *Taoist Meditation: The Mao-Shan Tradition of Great Purity*. Albany, NY: State University of New York Press.

Rosenthal, D. A., and S. S. Feldman. 1991. "The Influence of Perceived Family and Personal Factors on Self-Reported School Performance of Chinese and Western High School Students." *Journal of Research on Adolescence* 1: 135–154.

Salili, F., C. Y. Chiu, and S. Lai. 2001. "The Influence of Culture and Context on Students' Achievement Orientations." In *Student Motivation: The Culture and Context of Learning*, edited by F. Salili, C. Y. Chiu, and Y. Y. Hong, 221–247. New York, NY: Kluwer Academic/Plenum Press.

Spina, R., and L. J. Ji. 2011. "Cultural Differences in Curiosity." Unpublished manuscript, Department of Psychology, Queen's University, Canada.

Stevenson, H. W., and S. Lee. 1996. "The Academic Achievement of Chinese Students." In *The Handbook of Chinese Psychology*, edited by Michael H. Bond, 124–142. London, UK: Oxford University Press.

Stevenson, H. W., and J. W. Stigler. 1992. *The Learning Gap: Why Our Schools Are Failing and What We Can Learn from Japanese and Chinese Education*. New York, NY: Summit Books.

Tafarodi, R. W., T. C. Marshall, and H. Katsura. 2004. "Standing Out in Canada and Japan." *Journal of Personality* 72: 785–814.

Tweed, R. G., and D. R. Lehman. 2002. "Learning Considered within a Cultural Context: Confucian and Socratic Approaches." *American Psychologist* 57: 89–99.

Volet, S. 2001. "Significance of Cultural and Motivation Variables on Students' Attitudes towards Group Work." In *Student Motivation: The Culture and Context of Learning*, edited by F. Salili, C. Y. Chiu, and Y. Y. Hong, 309–333. New York, NY: Kluwer Academic/Plenum Press.

TIEYUAN GUO is an assistant professor in the Department of Psychology at the University of Macau, China.

2

This chapter explores the background and development of outcomes-based collaborative teaching and learning, and provides guidance for writing learning outcomes and engaging students in the Asian higher education context.

Outcomes-Based Collaborative Teaching and Learning in Asian Higher Education

Gertina J. van Schalkwyk

Engaging in collaborative knowledge construction needs careful designing, planning, and arranging the teaching and learning environment to guide students through the challenges and uncertainties of learning and lead them to develop the skills necessary to achieve success in the higher education context. Choreographing an outcomes-based collaborative teaching and learning (OBCTL) environment aims to move learning in higher education settings from the traditional content-based and input-driven teaching approaches (i.e., information transference) to an approach that is student-centered, holistic, and geared toward knowledge co-construction. All in all, OBCTL involves the art of planning and arranging a course starting with the course outline or learning contract, planning for the content and processes, and assessment of the educational experience. In this way, the instructor can fully engage students in co-constructing new meanings and methods for achieving educational goals and succeeding in life after university study.

The focus in this chapter is on the principles of instructional design and planning for effective OBCTL in a higher education settings. Although not specific to the Asian higher educational setting, the principles are easily transferable to contexts where the Confucian heritage culture (CHC) prevails (e.g., China, Japan, Southeast Asia). Thus, in this chapter, the characteristics of an outcomes-based education and collaborative teaching and learning are explored, setting the stage for effective instructional design and course planning that is engaging and pragmatic, also for Asian learners.

Outcomes-Based Education

Outcomes-based education (OBE) originated in the second half of the twentieth century and differs from traditional content-based and input-driven

NEW DIRECTIONS FOR TEACHING AND LEARNING, no. 142, Summer 2015 © 2015 Wiley Periodicals, Inc.
Published online in Wiley Online Library (wileyonlinelibrary.com) • DOI: 10.1002/tl.20128

approaches in the sense that those types of teaching and learning were mainly textbook driven and instructor centered (Pliner and Johnson 2004; Van der Horst and McDonald 2004). The aim of content-based learning was to master knowledge contained in the textbook—the source of knowledge—and the instructor assessed how well students could remember or recall the content. Input-driven teaching and learning aimed at transferring the knowledge to the student, usually through long lectures, while expecting the student to take notes, memorize, and recall the information in exact form and structure.

The roots of OBE lie in the 1950s with the movement toward setting educational objectives. Ralph Tyler (1949) identified the importance of formulating clearly defined objectives for the systematic planning of the learning experience with the focus on what the student should be able to do after completing the learning process and mastering the content. Subsequently, Bloom and colleagues (1956) developed the well-known Bloom's taxonomy to conceptualize the intellectual objectives aimed at expanding the cognitive domains involved in the learning process. The 1960s saw the emergence of competency-based education in the United States with the main purpose of ensuring the adequate preparation of students for a life after school. The focus was on integrating outcome goals, instructional experiences, and assessment devices to ensure understanding and enable all students to achieve the highest possible levels of learning of a particular skill or career. To this end, the instructor developed learning objectives geared toward demonstrable capabilities. Assessment was not to determine a grade per se but to ensure competency and to determine if more training was necessary. Firmly rooted in the constructivist paradigm, competency-based education supported the idea that learning was individual and that the individual needed to be goal oriented (Voorhees 2001; Weddel 2006).

Another predecessor of OBE was mastery learning, which placed the onus on the instructor and focused on providing suitable conditions for effective learning to occur. The aim of this approach was to provide sufficient learning opportunities for students to be successful, and the mastering of knowledge, skills, and attitudes provided important guidance for planning and implementing OBE (Van der Horst and McDonald 2004). The final predecessor that influenced OBE was the development of criteria-referenced assessment. This approach referred to testing in which students' grades were compared to a set standard that aimed at determining whether students have achieved the expected outcomes. Assessment became an ongoing process (continuous) that resulted in making adjustments in the teaching or instructional process and also provided students with guidance where improvements were necessary in order to be successful.

Although OBE initially focused only on what the students need to do (the outcomes of learning), later developments also referred to the teaching process involved in outcomes-based teaching and learning (OBTL) to ensure achievement of the outcomes. Van der Horst and McDonald (2004) and others (e.g., Biggs and Tang 2007) define OBTL as an approach that requires educators and students to focus their attention on the desired end result of each learning process and the instruction and learning processes that guide students to achieve these end results. Educators in this model were required to use the learning outcomes as a focus when they make instructional decisions, design assessments, and plan their lessons. More recently, Biggs and Tang (2007) differentiated between versions of OBTL and concluded that the teaching process involves three essential features: (1) the intended outcomes of teaching and learning stated at the start; (2) intended learning outcomes guide the teaching process and increase the likelihood that most students will achieve success; and (3) assessment should determine how well students achieve the outcomes. Therefore, the OBTL approach is student centered, and focuses equally on knowledge and skills and on the processes of teaching and optimizing the learning experience. The learning outcomes involve what students need to learn with regard to knowledge, skills, and attitudes or values. Lesson planning aims to assist students to achieve the outcomes, while continuous evaluation (formative assessment) of students' progress provides a demonstration of the achievement of these outcomes. Thus, OBTL focuses on *what students must be able to do or achieve during or at the end of a learning situation or section in order to attain the general objectives of the course.*

Furthermore, OBTL implies a paradigm shift toward supporting high levels of learning for all students. It comprises an approach that moves away from blaming students for lacking motivation or capabilities or blaming teachers for assumed inadequacies. Rather, it focuses on what students can do and how what students do relates to teaching (Biggs and Tang 2007). In the OBTL approach, the role of the instructor changes: The instructor should not *teach* but rather *facilitate* learning by stimulating a range of activities that will support the achievement of the learning outcomes. That is, the instructor should provide guidance for students to achieve their outcomes by choreographing specific learning activities and assessment tasks (Van Schalkwyk 2007). Therefore, determining the learning outcomes is the most important aspect of course planning, as the outcomes define the knowledge, skills, and attitudes that will guide the entire educational process. (See more about writing learning outcomes in the section titled "Writing Intended Learning Outcomes.") Knowledge and skills come from a range of sources, and learning should empower students through the achievement of outcomes as well as the assessment that guides and evaluates the learning process.

Outcomes-Based Collaborative Teaching and Learning

Collaborative teaching and learning (CTL) is an extension of OBE in that it refers to facilitating processes to motivate and engage students in educational activities that resonate with the learning outcomes and with students' everyday lives, future goals, and intended careers. In this regard, CTL focuses on the teaching and learning processes that connect to real-life situations and the ways outcomes are achieved in the real world. Combining OBE and CTL brings about the model for teaching and learning espoused in this chapter, namely OBCTL. OBCTL deviates from the conventional and traditional content-based education in the sense that it focuses on "knowledge as constructed in conjoint activities with others—in what people do together" (McNamee 2007, 314). The instructor and the student engage in processes of making meaning together and in mastering the processes linked to intended learning outcomes in order to achieve success both in the educational setting and in real-life contexts. The emphasis is therefore on relational practices and student-centered learning to its fullest extent.

OBCTL provides scope for mastering capabilities, knowledge, skills, techniques, and methods transferable to new situations. Students exposed to this approach have the benefit of developing skills, methods, techniques, and procedures that relate to real-life work. The educational experience empowers students through the achievement of outcomes as well as through the processes of learning, which include relational, emotive, social, and cognitive processes necessary for collaboration, self-reflection, and assessment, to achieve success in the world of work. Underlying this approach is the belief that collaborative efforts among all parties—that is, the instructor, the students, and the subject matter—are relevant in order to achieve intended learning outcomes for a program or course. CTL, when compared to cooperative teaching and learning (Dillenbourg 1999; Millis 2010), is less structured and more student oriented, resulting in greater effort by students while ensuring flexibility and expecting critical and reflective thinking and solutions not yet known to the instructor or the students. OBCTL requires improvisational choreography of the educational experience and the co-construction of knowledge in a relational context.

The OBCTL model also aligns well with what Chickering and Gamson (1987) proposed in their principles of student-centered teaching and learning, namely encouraging student–faculty contact, cooperation among students, and active learning; giving prompt (formative) feedback; emphasizing time on task; and communicating high expectations and respect for diverse talents and ways of learning. In my experience, these principles are quite effective in engendering deep learning in the Asian higher education setting. When integrating diverse strategies for OBCTL and engaging students in ways that encourage cooperation, active learning, time on task, and high expectations help to avoid resorting to punitive actions (i.e., negative reinforcement) and surface learning or passivity with which students in the CHC contexts are all too familiar (see Table 2.1).

Despite its flexibility on one hand, OBCTL also implies some structure within which to regulate the interaction within collaborating groups and

Table 2.1. Traditional Educational Experiences versus the OBCTL Experience

Traditional	New
Passive learners waiting for the input from the instructor	Active learners who prepare themselves for specific activities, interact with authentic problems and broader environments, and constructively engage with methods, materials, time management, technology, and equipment.
Learning is textbook/worksheet-bound and educator-centered	Learning is student-centered and instructor-facilitated, and both parties constantly perform and monitor tasks in order to achieve the outcomes.
Educators are responsible for learning; student motivation is dependent on the personality of the educator	Students take responsibility for their learning; engage in critical thinking, reasoning, reflection, and action; interact with the problem or assignment, peer group, and broader environment; and receive regular feedback and affirmation of their worth.
Exam-driven and rote learning	The outcome assessment is continuous until concluded or completed, entailing evaluation, checking, verification, rectifying, auditing, and commissioning of outcomes with a view to submitting it for assessment.
Emphasis is on what the educator hopes to achieve	Emphasis is on outcomes—what the student understands and can do—and on assessing all elements of the learning process by means of self-assessment, peer group assessment, instructor assessment, and client assessment.

to induce cognitive processes appropriate to group learning. The learning outcomes guide OBCTL and focus the teaching process on developing the social, emotional, and cognitive skills and attitudes necessary for producing deep learning. For deep learning to occur, achievement gains, critical thinking, problem solving, and reflective learning are important within the educational setting. Both the instructor and the student actively engage in structuring and regulating the processes involved in deep learning. Through the co-construction of knowledge and planned activities for individual effort and constructive competition, students acquire and apply knowledge and develop the skills to complete the task effectively and collaborate with others to achieve success (Johnson and Johnson 2009; Van der Horst and McDonald 2004).

Thus, OBCTL is a pragmatic approach to teaching and learning that values the effort students espouse when engaging in an educational setting. It aligns well with the expectations of success, social responsibility, and upward mobility instilled in many Asian students coming from Confucian heritage cultures (Phuong-Mai, Terlouw, and Pilot 2005). Shi (2006) claims that Chinese students, like Western students, value active learning and a more interactive relationship with teachers and peers. Although "westerners tend to see success as being attributable more to ability than to effort, [and] ethnic Chinese see effort as more important" (Biggs and Tang 2007, 33), OBCTL allows individuals and groups to excel in the educational context, applying both ability and effort.

Choreographing OBCTL.   In OBCTL, the focus is on choreographing a learning stage where joint activities, a range of social and cognitive processes, and interdependence evolve in ways applicable to success in life in general. Both ability and effort are important, and the aim is to guide students in the acquisition of skills needed to "apply" their knowledge in different settings in pursuit of solutions to problems. Through the co-construction of personal and public knowledge, strategies emerge that would sustain beyond the realms of the classroom and into the future. Instruction must therefore allow for learning experiences that go beyond the content, such as the application of rules and procedures, and find creative solutions to problems. Over and above mastering content and skills, students in the OBCTL model acquire competency to engage in constructive ways with knowledge by devising their own formulas or blueprints to achieve outcomes and apply the knowledge at an even higher level of complexity (Garrison and Archer 2000; Johnson and Johnson 2009; Van der Horst and McDonald 2004). However, it is a myth to claim that content is not important in OBCTL. One cannot do or demonstrate any skills without basic content knowledge. Students need to learn the facts (i.e., information) and also where to get the facts or information if needed. They also need to learn how to evaluate and question the facts and to discriminate between fact and fallacy. Ultimately, students need to learn how to use the facts, not merely to reproduce them. Thus, in a sound OBCTL environment, students will achieve the outcomes once they employ the supportive elements, learn the basics, and engage with others (the instructor, peers, and the broader context) in an interactive and collaborative manner (Van Offenbeek 2001).

In a well-choreographed OBCTL environment, students need to acquire the necessary supportive elements instrumental in achieving the outcomes and demonstrate the processes required to attain those outcomes. These supportive elements involve preparation, performance, interactions with others, completion of various tasks, and continuous assessment of progress and are intended to enable students to successfully achieve the outcomes of a course or program. The supportive elements are not outcomes. As an example, mastering content, as in *know and understand concepts of the discipline*, can never be an outcome, since the content alone is inherently inert, empty, and sterile. Rather, outcomes are end results of learning at a specific level, drawing on whatever embedded knowledge and content (i.e., the concepts of the discipline), skills, and supportive processes are required for demonstrating achievement of the outcomes. The outcomes point to what students should know and be able to do after completing the course, participating in class discussions, reading, and performing various learning tasks such as reading, explaining, applying, reflecting, problem solving, and relating to principles. As a student-centered approach, OBCTL thus aims to assist students to undertake appropriate learning activities that will ensure not only surface learning but also deep learning at the desired levels of engagement (Phuong-Mai, Terlouw, and Pilot 2005).

Key Elements of Course Design and Planning for OBCTL

The previous explication of the background and emergence of OBCTL sets the stage for designing learning experiences in a higher education context. There are multiple examples in the literature of how to effectively design and plan a learning program in OBCTL (e.g., Biggs and Tang 2007; Dijkstra et al. 1997; Pliner and Johnson 2004; Wiggins and McTighe 2005). Most of the examples take a systematic approach involving five key elements—analysis, planning and conceptualizing, conducting, assessment, and reflecting. The first element entails an analysis of the context in which teaching and learning will take place—that is, the institutional, departmental, and classroom resources and facilities. In this regard, one has to analyze the needs that a particular course will have to fulfill within the broader learning program as well as the student body and its degree of diversity or homogeneity. Knowledge of Asian students and their characteristic ways of learning in a Confucian heritage culture is imperative to ensure successful OBCTL.

Closely linked to the analysis is the planning and conceptualizing of a course in OBCTL. This element refers primarily to the writing of specific learning outcomes as the end product of the learning experience and the constructive alignment of these outcomes with strategies for facilitating the achievement of the outcomes. The aim is to plan the course in such a way that it will resonate with students' expectations of learning; ensure their achievement of the necessary knowledge, skills, and attitudes to demonstrate success with the envisioned outcomes; and ensure that learning takes place at the deepest level. The rest of this chapter focuses on writing learning outcomes in OBCTL and aligning the outcomes with assessment strategies. The reader should also read Chapter 3 for more ways of conducting OBCTL.

In the planning for a course, the instructor begins with envisioning the objectives or goals that he or she wants to achieve as the end product of teaching and learning. The objective of a course is a simple statement of what the instructor hopes to achieve with the instructional design and involves aligning the course goal with the expected outcomes of the study program in which the course fits. Thus, the course objective involves the discipline-specific knowledge and content that will motivate and engage students as well as providing a practical and useful reason for why they should study the specific program. The objective also provides a conceptual framework (e.g., theory, theme, and controversial issues) that will support the content and engage students in required higher-order learning activities and enduring understanding. *Maintaining a learner-centered and process-oriented approach, one can ask what the students need to know and do in order to derive maximum benefit from the educational experience.*

Whereas the objective for the course describes the overall content and context of the learning experience, the learning outcomes refer to achievements expected of students and draw on specific knowledge and skills, displayed in a particular context and demonstrated and evaluated as clearly observable end products of learning. In this sense, the learning outcomes involve the methods, techniques, and procedures that relate to real-life work and that can be repeated in new contexts. Rather than the traditional approach of defining topics that need to be covered, the focus is on designing intended learning outcomes that will ensure enduring understanding (Biggs and Tang 2007; Wiggins and McTighe 2005). Learning outcomes include not only the content that is worth covering but, more important, the elements of the learning process that have enduring value beyond the classroom. The instructor considers not only the course objective captured in the course description but also the learning outcomes that should endure over the long term.

In OBCTL, the design and planning culminate in *a course outline* that serves as a contract of learning between instructor and student. The course outline is sometimes referred to as the syllabus, and, similar to a syllabus, it guides the planning and design of a course as a unique learning experience aimed at achieving the desired outcomes or results (Biggs and Tang 2007; Pliner and Johnson 2004). The course outline provides some structure in terms of what students have to prepare and complete (i.e., reading about the topic or theme) and when assignments are due. Contrary to the traditional concept of a syllabus, the course outline in OBCTL is not content driven, broken down into subjects or themes, and rigid and nonnegotiable. Rather, the course outline is a more integrative document that provides all components relevant to the learning experience—a comprehensive contract of learning that integrates the intended learning outcomes (ILOs), assessment tasks, and instructional strategies. Therefore, careful planning and preparation of the course outline are important; without proper planning and preparation, instructors will not be able to teach in this model.

Writing Intended Learning Outcomes

The next step is to conceptualize the critical and specific learning outcomes that will guide the instructional process and assessment strategies. Prior to writing a learning outcome, one needs to understand that *knowledge, skills, standards, performances, objectives, courses, modules,* and *goals* are *not* interchangeable terms for the word "outcome." Outcomes or ILOs refer to achievements expected of students and draw on specific knowledge and skills, displayed in a particular context and demonstrated and evaluated as clearly observable end products of learning (Van der Horst and McDonald 2004). The ILOs point to what students should know and be able to do after completing the course, participating in class discussions, reading, and performing in projects of learning or assignments. Students who meet the criteria for achieving the ILOs for a course will qualify for a credit of some kind. In order to qualify for a credit, students should be capable of demonstrating that they can achieve the ILOs at specific levels of understanding.

There are two kinds of learning outcomes: *critical cross-field outcomes* and *specific outcomes* (Olivier 1998; Van der Horst and McDonald 2004). *Critical cross-field outcomes* are usually designed by the program and apply to all the learning areas within the field or discipline in the program of study. The aim of critical outcomes is to direct educational activities toward development of students within the broader learning environment of the program (or major) they enrolled for. Thus, critical outcomes are generic and cross-curricular and are linked or aligned to all levels of the program and the institutional vision in general (Biggs and Tang 2007). Achievement of critical outcomes will also ensure that students gain the knowledge, skills, and values that will allow them to demonstrate scholarship (i.e., academic knowledge, competence, and openness to inquiry), global citizenship (i.e., societal responsibilities and obligations), and lifelong learning (i.e., committed to continuous learning and reflection and dealing with new problems and issues as they arise). Critical outcomes also involve the *attributes* that students should acquire upon completion of a program. Most accreditation bodies require institutions to develop critical outcomes for the programs they offer and to provide evidence or assurance of learning that these outcomes have been achieved when the students complete the program (see Figure 2.1). Note that the attributes (or competences) students should develop are not ILOs but provide the basis for conceptualizing the critical outcomes.

Specific outcomes, the second kind of outcomes, are the ILOs that an instructor develops when planning for the course. The main point of writing specific outcomes is to ensure that the course ILOs support students to achieve the critical outcomes for the program as a whole. These specific outcomes are achievements within a specific context of the course, and express the results or performance of narrowly defined aspects of learning required for the course. Specific outcomes also involve the supportive

Figure 2.1. Critical Outcomes at Program Level

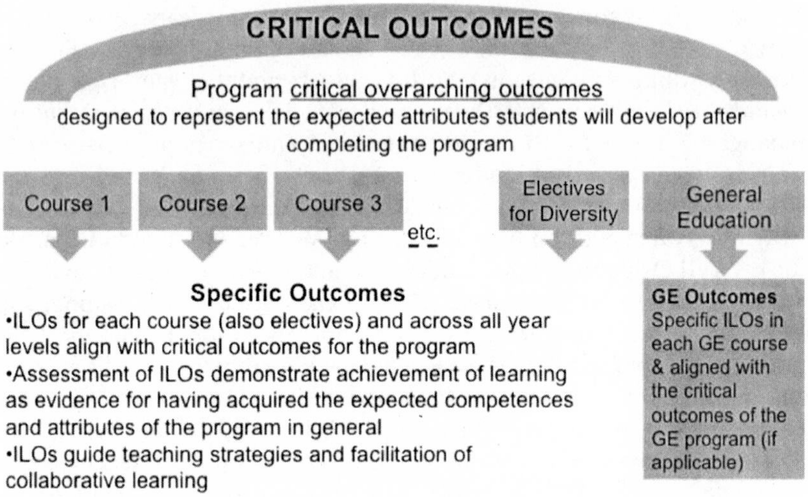

CRITICAL OUTCOMES

Program <u>critical overarching outcomes</u>
designed to represent the expected attributes students will develop after
completing the program

Course 1	Course 2	Course 3		Electives for Diversity	General Education

etc.

Specific Outcomes
•ILOs for each course (also electives) and across all year
levels align with critical outcomes for the program
•Assessment of ILOs demonstrate achievement of learning
as evidence for having acquired the expected competences
and attributes of the program in general
•ILOs guide teaching strategies and facilitation of
collaborative learning

GE Outcomes
Specific ILOs in
each GE course
& aligned with
the critical
outcomes of the
GE program (if
applicable)

elements for acquiring the kind knowledge, topics of interest, and levels of understanding within the course. The specific outcomes are context-linked achievements students should be able to demonstrate in particular areas of learning (i.e., a course) at a specific level of competence. Together, the specific outcomes and assessment criteria are supportive of the achievements of credits and qualifications, and provide a framework for assurance of learning.

Writing ILOs in OBCTL requires careful planning. It is advisable not to have more than seven outcomes for the course and often fewer for each lesson within the course. ILOs comprise a specification of the embedded knowledge, skills, values, and/or attitudes that a student is expected to acquire within a given discipline or field of study. The function of ILOs is twofold: (1) They enable the instructor to know in advance what students are expected to know and do; and (2) they enable students to know in advance what they will be expected to know and do or achieve. Therefore, an effective learning outcome indicates these points:

• Who is to perform?
• What task is to be performed?
• What conditions, if any, apply at the time of assessment?
• What is the minimum response required to indicate mastery of the task?

ILOs should be written in unambiguous language, using action verbs that have clear meanings, and should involve more than mere isolated tasks or skills. They should describe the student's performance in terms of observable, demonstrable and assessable actions, decisions, or services. An ILO

Figure 2.2. Components of Writing ILO

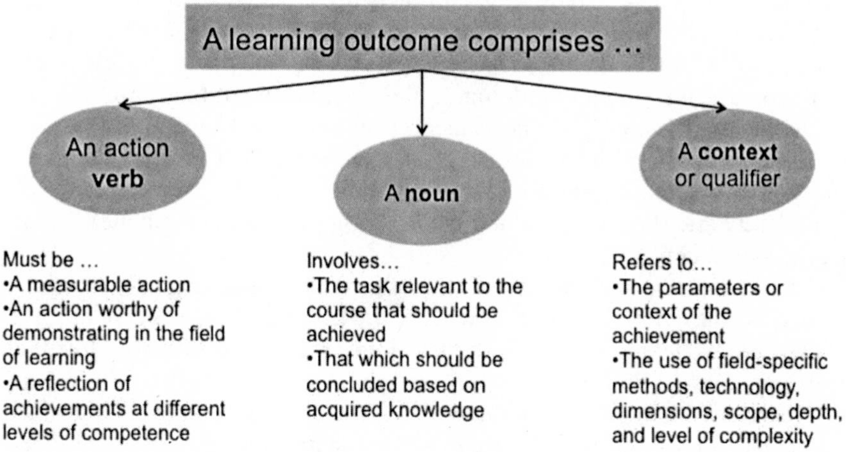

A learning outcome comprises ...

An action verb

A noun

A context or qualifier

Must be ...
•A measurable action
•An action worthy of demonstrating in the field of learning
•A reflection of achievements at different levels of competence

Involves...
•The task relevant to the course that should be achieved
•That which should be concluded based on acquired knowledge

Refers to...
•The parameters or context of the achievement
•The use of field-specific methods, technology, dimensions, scope, depth, and level of complexity

always involves consideration of three key components: (1) the kind of action to perform with available knowledge (i.e., the verb); (2) the task or aspect relevant to the course area that should be achieved (i.e., the noun/object); and (3) the intended level of understanding or complexity of the achievement (i.e., the qualifier) (e.g., Biggs and Tang 2007). Figure 2.2 summarizes the three components of ILOs. Each component is further explained next.

When writing ILOs, the *verb* signifies the activity that is going to take place, for example, *describe* a procedure, *compile* a budget, *solve* a problem, *identify* and *explain* the learning styles. In a sense, the verb indicates the characteristics of the outcome, since compiling a budget differs from auditing a budget. Not all verbs are amenable to use. Verbs such as "understand," "appreciate," or "possess" are passive verbs and difficult to measure or observe as evidence that learning has taken place. These verbs do not describe what the end result or outcome will be and therefore are not appropriate to use as outcomes-based terminology. Some action verbs do imply a range of actions that embody the envisioned attributes set as critical outcomes for the program. For example, in order to "explain," "critique," "compare," "describe," or "review," the student will have to exhibit analytical skills, critical thinking, and various communication skills. Thus, an ILO such as *"explain how knowledge of different approaches to human development can enhance well-being"* implicitly refers to the knowledge underlying human development, analytical skills for comparing different approaches, and written or oral modes of communication—the student cannot explain anything without having developed appropriate skills.

The *noun/object* spells out what is going to be achieved (e.g., a procedure, a budget, a mechanical/technical problem, or the learning styles). It names and limits the issue or topic to be addressed and the knowledge area that has to be accessed in order to complete the task. Thus, the noun/object specifies the task, relevant to and dependent on learning in the field of study (i.e., knowledge), that should be concluded. The *qualifier* or *context* refers to the parameters and methodologies of the achievement (e.g., a procedure *in counseling*, a budget *for a new business venture*, a mechanical problem *in building construction*, or learning styles *in a primary school setting*). The qualifiers or modifiers, as they are sometimes called, also describe the range of complexity and the level at which the learning outcomes are pitched—that is, the assessment criteria.

Since the verb indicates what the essence of the learning process envisioned for the course or program will be, the list of ILOs in a course outline encapsulates the end results of the learning process and forms part of the learning contract between a student and the instructor—what the student will learn and do to provide evidence of learning (i.e., assessment) and what the instructor will do to facilitate the learning and the activities for different lessons to ensure the outcomes can be achieved (i.e., teaching). Active verbs in the ILOs also reflect different levels of understanding and cognitive functioning (Biggs and Tang 2007). A classical list or taxonomy of active verbs for writing outcomes is Bloom's taxonomy, which reflects the different cognitive domains necessary to achieve the envisioned outcomes. Bloom's taxonomy has been in use for many decades, and Anderson and Krathwohl (2001) present the most up-to-date and comprehensive classification according to six cognitive domains relevant to learning at higher education level. Anderson and Krathwohl provide an easily accessible taxonomy of the cognitive processes and action verbs that are useful when conceptualising ILOs in each of the six categories.

Other taxonomies categorize emotional domains (Krathwohl, Bloom, and Masia 1964), levels of moral development (Good and Brophy 1990), and psychomotor domains for courses in physical education, art, and the performing arts (Harrow 1972). Biggs and Collis (1982) devised a structure for the observed learning outcome (SOLO). The SOLO taxonomy systematically describes how a student's performance should grow in complexity through the mastering of various academic tasks and gives a list of verbs that indicate "what the students need to be able to do to indicate achievement at the level in question" (Biggs and Tang 2007, 79). In their exposition of the SOLO taxonomy, Biggs and Collis also refer to the quantitative and qualitative stages of learning that should occur over time as the student engages in the course or learning program. The quantitative stage relates to learning of detail, such as the specific knowledge aspects involved in a course, while the qualitative stage relates to the integration of the detail in more advanced levels of application and thus guides the assessment strategies that one can use to gain evidence of learning. The taxonomies provide cues for conceptualizing ILOs. In higher education, ILOs should focus on the higher-order

Table 2.2. "Exploring the Earth" Course Description

Course Title	Exploring the Earth
Course description	This course is an introduction to the basic concepts of physical science. Students completing this course will gain an introductory understanding of the major principles of physical geology covering the structure of the earth, plate tectonics, volcanism and other mountain-building processes, the surface erosion process, and the formation and properties of minerals and rocks.
Intended learning outcomes (ILOs)	After completing this course, students should be able to:
	1. Identify and classify major geological structures when reading and interpreting maps, graphs, tables, and diagrams of physical geology.
	2. Report and discuss key processes for the formation of the major physical structures covering the earth.
	3. Select the relevant principles to solve problems of surface erosion.
	4. Present analyses and results of experiments in a written report and oral presentation using appropriate and effective language and media.
	5. Conceptualize and act upon the group and individual dynamics and their impact on the physical geology covering the structure of the earth.

cognitive domains, such as apply, analyze, evaluate, and create, and more advanced levels of abstraction.

As an example of writing ILOs for a course, I present here a case of a course in "Exploring the Earth" (Table 2.2). The example includes the course description (objective) and ILOs that comprise a specification of the knowledge, skills, values, and attitudes a student is expected to acquire in a given learning area within a discipline or field of study (Van der Horst and McDonald 2004). The ILOs indicate what the student is required to do under specific conditions by applying the knowledge embedded in the discipline or course.

In the example, the ILOs represent the active verbs relevant to two kinds of knowledge (i.e., declarative knowledge and functioning knowledge) and different levels of understanding (i.e., unistructural, multistructural, and relational) included in the SOLO model (see Biggs and Tang 2007). *Declarative knowledge* is knowledge that is abstract and conceptual, dealing with knowing about things. It usually refers to content knowledge accrued from reading and research and not from personal experience or application. Active verbs such as "identify," "classify," "select," and "conceptualize" in the ILOs refer to knowing about the concepts, principles, and processes of physical geology. Knowledge about the subject matter or content is therefore embedded in the ILOs.

Functioning (or professional) knowledge refers to specific and pragmatic knowledge and is underpinned by understanding the subject matter. It is knowledge within the experience of the learner who uses declarative (theoretical) knowledge to perform certain tasks, such as solving problems, analyzing results, or discussing key processes in the ILOs for the course example just presented. Some topics require a deeper level of understanding. Students need to know about the concepts and principles (embedded knowledge) and understand at a level that allows them to put their knowledge to work. Topics need to be stated in terms of what the students are required to do, not what you the instructor have to cover in class or set as required reading (Biggs and Tang 2007).

In summary, when writing ILOs for a course, one has to carefully consider each of the three key components:

1. the kind of knowledge involved (declarative or functioning);
2. the content or topic to be learned; and
3. the level of understanding or performance to be achieved.

When writing the course ILOs, the instructor will translate the intended level of understanding or performance as an outcome (active) verb and the topic in which the verb is to be enacted. The kind of knowledge is embedded in the active verb and the topic and need not be explicit in the ILO. The instructor decides on this in her or his planning to help clarify thinking and decision making when writing the ILOs. To recap a course ILO from the previous example, students should be able to: *Identify* and *classify* (i.e., the level of understanding and performance) *major geological structures* (i.e., the noun or content within the field) *when reading and interpreting maps, graphs, tables, and diagrams of physical geology* (i.e., context and qualifier).

Assessment Standards for ILOs

The ILOs should also describe the standard at which the student should demonstrate the achievement of learning and the degree (depth and breadth) of demonstrating the achievement (Van der Horst and McDonald 2004; Wiggins and McTighe 2005). This comprises the assessment standard that contributes toward the qualification. Assessment standards are grade specific and show how conceptual progression will occur. They embody the knowledge, skills, and values required to achieve the learning outcomes but do not prescribe the method. Assessment standards are also included in the course outline as rubrics to help students make judgments about their own performance, set goals for progress, and encourage further learning. The instructor chooses or selects the evidence that will be used to determine that students have understood the content.

Standard setting for acceptable evidence comprises three types of assessment (Wiggins and McTighe 2005):

1. The *performance task* is at the heart of the learning and is meant to be a real-world challenge in the thoughtful and effective use of knowledge and skills—an authentic test of understanding in context.
2. *Criteria referenced assessment* involves regular or continuous tasks such as quizzes, term papers, reflections, and various in-class and out-of-class learning projects that provide the instructor and student with timely feedback on how well the facts and concepts are being understood and applied in different contexts.
3. *Unprompted assessment* and *self-assessment* engage the student actively in achieving the learning outcomes and are used to make adjustments in order to achieve the required standards of learning.

OBCTL in Asian Higher Education

Throughout the process of planning and preparing for a course, it is important to keep in mind how the three components—ILOs, assessment, and instructional strategies—align to facilitate and enhance the teaching and learning environment and ensure that students achieve success. Other chapters in this volume expand on the instructional strategies and assessment tasks and discuss how to adapt these when teaching in an Asian context. The reader is also encouraged to access Biggs and Tang (2007) and similar texts that provide a framework for constructive alignment of outcomes, assessment tasks (or projects of learning), and teaching or learning activities.

The OBCTL model challenges both instructors and students to "reconstruct how they think about teaching and learning" (Anderson 2002, 2) and about sharing responsibility for the learning process as equal partners. The shift toward new ways of thinking about learning, and particularly toward OBCTL in higher education settings, is often more challenging to the Asian student coming from a Confucian heritage culture. Prior learning experiences that suppressed active involvement and the co-construction of problem solving and new knowledge often restrict Asian students in the OBCTL model. It is a fallacy to think that Asian students automatically know how to collaborate toward successful completion of a learning task. On one hand, they are highly motivated toward individual accountability and competitive when striving for grades. On the other hand, Asian students place a high value on harmony and the avoidance of conflict (i.e., argumentation). The Confucian heritage culture also defines the positioning of instructor and student in an almost nonnegotiable power hierarchy (Van Schalkwyk 2007). Asian students employing different rules of interpretation and cognitive processes (Nisbett 2003) and learning in their second language (e.g., English) often find it difficult to express their views in a nonnative language in which they may not feel that they are able to converse competently. Sharing in the process of knowledge co-construction seems almost a violation of their existing "realities," and engaging in conversational activity and talk as required for OBCTL is an unfamiliar concept to most students in an Asian higher education setting (Biggs and Tang 2007).

Understanding the Asian Student. In the student-centered approach underpinning OBCTL, the focus is on the student rather than the instructor. Students are required to construct and co-construct knowledge that is negotiated among members of the group or learning community rather than merely receiving or assimilating knowledge (Van Offenbeek 2001). This requires input from the students. Thus, an instructor coming from a Western-oriented teaching and learning environment needs to know the students that he or she will be teaching. Merely "transplanting" teaching models from non-Asian contexts (e.g., Western pedagogies) to the Asian context is inappropriate and often unsuccessful. Although Asian students are predisposed to issues such as interrelatedness, social orientation, and expending effort in their educational activities, they still need guidance to ensure success in collaborating with others to co-construct knowledge and solve problems. Table 2.3 summarizes some of the key differences between Asian and non-Asian students (Phuong-Mai, Terlouw, and Pilot 2005).

Despite some apparent differences between Asian and non-Asian students, Shi (2006, 122) claims that "contemporary Chinese students demonstrate different characteristics from those described in many previous studies" and that they "show little difference from their Western counterparts by being active learners and preferring a more interactive relationships with their teachers." Li and Campbell (2008) also found that Asian students value the significance of group discussions, particularly when engaging in their nonnative language (e.g., English). Nonetheless, Phuong-Mai, Terlouw, and Pilot (2005) also claim that Asian students hold intensely negative views about group work. In particular, they hold strong beliefs about the value of individual effort and perseverance and find it difficult to deal with factors contributing to group dynamics and the competing demands on students' time and attention. They are used to having model answers given to them in their secondary school, and in the higher education context, there are times when they are really dissatisfied with the fact that instructors do not give them the absolute model answers.

Harlene Anderson (2002) asserts that there should be room for the familiar when exploring new ideas, and the instructor who facilitates OBCTL has to know her or his students and how they learn as well as the cultural context in which they have learned in the past and will work in the future. Getting to know one's students and the Confucian heritage culture context in which they grew up is imperative in order for the instructor to "(a) access every members' creativity and resources and foster the kind of environment

Table 2.3. The Asian versus the Non-Asian Student

	Asian Student Raised in a Confucian Heritage Culture	Non-Asian Student Raised within Individualist Culture
Power distance	Expects and accepts the hierarchy rules in which power is distributed unequally in instructor–student and student–student relationships—that is, the instructor has more power (e.g., expert knowledge) and should model correct behavior. Students should be obedient, rarely question the instructor or the textbook, and remain dependent on the teacher for modeling the correct knowledge. The instructor is treated with deference even when no longer a student.	Accepts that power is distributed equally in the instructor–student and student–student relationships where both contribute equally to knowledge co-construction and shared leadership when participating as a team (Johnson and Johnson, 1994)—that is, although treating the instructor with respect, the student is not solely dependent on the instructor and eagerly challenges existing knowledge systems (and the instructor) in order to co-construct new knowledge.
Uncertainty avoidance	Prefers a high amount of structure, well-structured tasks, and linear thinking, limiting creative efforts.	Comfortable with a low amount of structure for tasks and critical thinking that enhances creative efforts.
Orientation toward time	A fluid time value and more likely to practice the eventual or long-term reciprocity norm—that is, the long-term orientation makes it difficult to cope with the pressure of time associated with participation in classroom group work (i.e., starting immediately) and postponing efforts for homework assignments (e.g., writing papers) to the last minute.	A more linear approach to time and more likely to practice a short-term time orientation—that is, the short-term orientation allows enthusiastic participation in classroom group work and attempting homework assignments (e.g., writing papers) sooner rather than later.
Interdependence-independence	People are integrated into strong, cohesive in-groups that continue to protect them throughout their lifetime in exchange for unquestioning loyalty.	The ties between individuals are loose, and everyone is expected to look after themselves and their immediate interests.

(Continued)

Table 2.3. Continued

	Asian Student Raised in a Confucian Heritage Culture	Non-Asian Student Raised within Individualist Culture
Gender stereotypes	Gender roles are clearly distinct, with men assertive, tough, and focused on material success and women modest, tender, and concerned with the quality of life.	Gender roles are less distinct, and both men and women are assertive and modest, tough and concerned with the quality of life.
Academic performance	Values academic performance. Competitive and grade oriented with the aim of achieving high marks and ranking among peers to bring prestige to the family.	Competitive in terms of achieving high marks but also tends to value independent thinking and autonomy in the process of learning.

in which each participant feels comfortable, open, and part of the conversations, and (b) to create spaces and relationships in which each person has a sense of freedom and belonging, spaces in which everyone can voice their ideas, ask questions, and express concerns, without feeling blamed or judged" (London and Rodriguez-Jazcilevich 2007, 238).

Thus, in the planning stage for a course or program, the instructor does not only envision what students need to know and do (i.e., knowledge, skills, and attitudes) in order to derive maximum benefit from the learning experience. The instructor should also acquaint him- or herself with the local culture and ways of being to ensure best practices for teaching and learning. Knowledge of how the Asian student perceives power and gender, values loyalty to the in group, avoids uncertainty, and perceives time orientation and intellectual effort could help the Western-trained instructor to adapt more successfully in the host culture. This knowledge also provides the instructor with a better understanding of how to engage Asian students when attempting to create a learning community with them. Creating community with Asian students and getting them to buy in requires acceptance of their unique characteristics and building up their confidence and respecting their unique heritage. However, in higher education settings, it is also important that students engage in discovering that they can think independently, analyze, and eventually understand concepts through engaging with peers in a learning community. Students have to accept responsibility for both individual and group learning and to participate in co-constructing new knowledge that goes beyond the scope of textbook materials and the instructor's expertise.

Western-Trained Instructor in the Asian Higher Education Context. Apart from knowing the student, the instructor also needs to know him- or herself and to reflect on how to develop a culturally responsive and caring OBCTL environment. In this regard, five points are relevant for consideration.

1. *Understanding one's own motives.* It is important that the Western-trained instructor understands his or her own motives, beliefs, biases, values, and assumptions about human behavior and recognizes his or her own ethnocentrism. In an Asian context, one's personal and professional assumptions and biases could be challenged. Therefore, an awareness of one's own societal values and beliefs and a systematic examination of how group affiliation influences one's sense of self in relation to others are important (Weinstein, Tomlinson-Clarke, and Curran 2004).

2. *Knowing how Asian students came to be.* Culturally responsive OBCTL requires knowledge of how the students developed over time, their family backgrounds, educational experiences, and cultural norms and values. One also needs to learn what questions are appropriate and how interactions—both positive and negative—between the instructor and students should be negotiated. For example, Weinstein, Tomlinson-Clarke, and Curran (2004, 26) comment that "Southeast Asian students smile while being scolded if they are unaware that the smiles are meant not as disrespect, but as an admission of guilt and an effort to show that there are no hard feelings."

3. *Understanding the context.* An understanding of the broader social, economic, and political context and how the norms of dominant groups became institutionalized helps one to recognise how differences in race, social class, gender, language background, and sexual orientation are linked to power and to the privileging of some groups while marginalizing others.

4. *Reflecting on taken-for-granted assumptions.* Awareness of one's own taken-for-granted assumptions, knowledge of the students' cultural backgrounds, and an understanding of the broader context assist the Western-trained instructor engaging in an Asian higher education context to reflect on her or his ability and willingness to use culturally appropriate classroom management strategies. For example, "reprimanding Chinese students for not being willing to express their opinions may conflict with their parents' directive to listen and learn what the teacher tells them" (Weinstein, Tomlinson-Clarke, and Curran 2004, 32). One also needs to reflect critically on one's behavior, equitable treatment, traditional assumptions of what works in classroom management, and ways of developing mutual accommodation when preparing and teaching in an Asian context.

5. *Choreographing a caring learning environment.* In OBCTL within an Asian context, the Western-trained instructor should commit to choreographing a caring classroom environment and should aim to create relationships grounded in cooperation, collaboration, and reciprocity rather than patterns of the teacher controlling student compliance. The aim is to grant "privilege and honour [to] the personal experiences, desires, motivations, knowledge and skills" (Carlson and Erickson 2001, 207) of students and to create a caring learning community in which students feel respected, trusted, and supported by the instructor and by one another.

Conclusion

This chapter reviewed the literature on outcomes-based and collaborative teaching and learning to set the stage for choreographing the teaching and learning environment in an Asian higher education setting. Choreographing in the OBCTL context refers to the rhythmic dance evolving in the interaction between instructor and students in an educational setting. As in dance or any other event, the choreographer or director guides the performers through their paces, often training them in specific skill sets and with the goal of staging a successful performance. Expecting performers to put on the play without guidance or minimal directions would be unsatisfactory—they need the guidance and have to practice the skills to ensure success. Similarly, the instructor in a higher education setting facilitates the collaborative actions and co-actions aimed at achieving the intended learning outcomes. Merely asking students to work together as a team or assigning a group task without careful planning and understanding of the intricate dynamics underlying OBCTL will not succeed. The reader is encouraged to also read the strategies for doing OBCTL in other chapters in this volume and to explore specific attributes that students should develop to successfully achieve the critical and specific outcomes of a program and course.

References

Anderson, H. 2002. "Supervision as a Collaborative Learning Community." *Music Therapy Today.* http://www.wfmt.info/Musictherapyworld/startup/MTT2000-3.pdf.

Anderson, L. W., and D. R. Krathwohl, eds. 2001. *A Taxonomy for Learning, Teaching and Assessing: A Revision of Bloom's Taxonomy of Educational Objectives.* New York, NY: Longman.

Biggs, J., and K. F. Collis. 1982. *Evaluating the Quality of Learning: The SOLO Taxonomy.* New York, NY: Academic Press.

Biggs, J., and C. Tang. 2007. *Teaching for Quality Learning at University*, 3rd ed. New York, NY: McGraw-Hill.

Bloom, B. S., M. D. Engelhart, E. J. Furst, W. H. Hill, and D. R. Krathwohl. 1956. *Taxonomy of Educational Objectives: The Classification of Educational Goals. Handbook I: Cognitive Domain.* New York: Longmans Green.

Carlson, T. D., and M. J. Erickson. 2001. "Honoring and Privileging Personal Experience and Knowledge." *Contemporary Family Therapy* 23: 199–220.

Chickering, A. W., and Z. F. Gamson. 1987. "Seven Principles for Good Practice in Undergraduate Education." *AAHE Bulletin* March: 2–6. http://files.eric.ed.gov/fulltext/ED282491.pdf.

Dijkstra, S., N. Seel, F. Schott, and R. D. Tennyson, eds. 1997. *Instructional Design: International Perspective*. Mahwah, NJ: Lawrence Erlbaum.

Dillenbourg, P., ed. 1999. *Collaborative Learning: Cognitive and Computational Approaches*. Oxford, UK: Elsevier.

Garrison, D. R., and W. Archer. 2000. *A Transactional Perspective on Teaching and Learning: A Framework for Adult and Higher Education*. Amsterdam, the Netherlands: Pergamon Press.

Good, T. L., and J. E. Brophy. 1990. *Educational Psychology: A Realistic Approach*. New York, NY: Longmans.

Harrow, A. J. 1972. *A Taxonomy of the Psychomotor Domain: A Guide for Developing Behavioural Objectives*. New York, NY: David McKay.

Johnson, D. W., and R. T. Johnson. 2009. "An Educational Psychology Success Story: Social Interdependence Theory and Cooperative Learning." *Educational Researchers* 38: 365–379.

Krathwohl, D. R., B. S. Bloom, and B. B. Masia. 1964. *Taxonomy of Educational Objectives. Handbook II: Affective Domain*. New York, NY: David McKay.

Li, M., and J. Campbell. 2008. "Asian Students' Perceptions of Group Work and Group Assignments in a New Zealand Tertiary Institution." *Intercultural Education* 19: 203–216.

London, S., and I. Rodriguez-Jazcilevich. 2007. "The Development of a Collaborative Learning and Therapy Community in an Educational Setting: From Alienation to Invitation." In *Collaborative Therapy: Relationships and Conversations That Make a Difference*, edited by H. Anderson and D. Gehart, 235–268. New York, NY: Routledge.

McNamee, S. 2007. "Relational Practices in Education: Teaching as Conversation." In *Collaborative Therapy: Relationships and Conversations That Make a Difference*, edited by H. Anderson and D. Gehart, 313–336. New York, NY: Routledge.

Millis, B. J., ed. 2010. *Cooperative Learning in Higher Education*. Sterling, VA: Stylus Publishing.

Nisbett, R. E. 2003. *The Geography of Thought*. London, UK: Free Press.

Olivier, C. 1998. *How to Educate and Train: Outcomes-Based*. Pretoria, South Africa: J. L. van Schaik.

Phuong-Mai, N., C. Terlouw, and A. Pilot. 2005. "Cooperative Learning vs. Confucian Heritage Culture's Collectivism: Confrontation to Reveal Some Cultural Conflicts and Mismatch." *Asia Europe Journal* 3: 403–419.

Pliner, S. M., and J. R. Johnson. 2004. "Historical, Theoretical and Foundational Principles of Universal Instructional Design in Higher Education." *Equity and Excellence in Education* 37: 105–113.

Shi, L. 2006. "The Successors to Confucianism or a New Generation?" *Language, Culture and Curriculum* 19: 122–147.

Tyler, R. W. 1949. *Basic Principles of Curriculum and Instruction*. Chicago, IL: University of Chicago Press.

Van der Horst, H., and R. McDonald. 2004. *Outcomes-Based Education: Theory and Practice*. Centurion, South Africa: Tee Vee Printers and Publishers.

Van Offenbeek, M. 2001. "Processes and Outcomes of Team Learning." *European Journal of Work and Organizational Psychology* 10: 303–317.

Van Schalkwyk, G. J. 2007. "Choreographing Learning in Developmental Psychology Utilising Multigenerational Genograms and Reflective Journal Writing." *International Education Journal* 8: 127–138.

Voorhees, R. A. 2001. "Competency-Based Learning Models: A Necessary Future." In *Measuring What Matters: Competency-Based Learning Models in Higher Education,* New Directions for Institutional Research, no. 201, edited by R. A. Voorhees, 5–13. San Francisco, CA: Jossey-Bass.

Weddel, K. S. 2006. *Competency-Based Education and Content Standards.* Northern Colorado Literacy Resource Center. http://www.d11.org/Transition/iep/Documents/CompetencyBasedEducation.pdf.

Weinstein, C. S., S. Tomlinson-Clarke, and M. Curran. 2004. "Toward a Conception of Culturally Responsive Classroom Management." *Journal of Teacher Education* 55: 25–38.

Wiggins, G., and J. McTighe. 2005. *Understanding by Design,* 2nd ed. Alexandria, VA: Association for Supervision and Curriculum Development.

GERTINA J. VAN SCHALKWYK *is an associate professor of psychology and head of the Department of Psychology, and former coordinator for professional development in the Centre for Teaching and Learning Enhancement at the University of Macau, China.*

NEW DIRECTIONS FOR TEACHING AND LEARNING • DOI: 10.1002/tl

3

This chapter focuses on applying the concepts of outcomes-based collaborative teaching and learning in an Asian context and with students coming from a Confucian heritage culture and explores examples of how to implement effective collaborative teaching and learning in an Asian higher education setting.

Doing Outcomes-Based Collaborative Teaching and Learning in Asia

Gertina J. van Schalkwyk

In outcomes-based collaborative teaching and learning (OBCTL), the focus is on choreographing a learning stage where joint activities, a range of social and cognitive processes, and interdependence evolve in ways applicable to success in life in general. Both ability and effort are important, and the aim is to guide students in the acquisition of skills needed to apply their knowledge in different settings in pursuit of solutions to problems. OBCTL involves motivation and engagement to fully absorb students in creating meanings through personal experience, interpretation, and application of the knowledge they acquire in the learning environment. Planning and arranging activities in OBCTL involves the art of choreographing sequences of in-class and out-of-class actions, interactions, and co-actions that are motivational and engaging as well as resonate with the everyday lives of students and the world of work. The focus is on enhancing the teaching and learning environment and facilitating the transfer of knowledge, attitude, and skills in such a manner that students can appreciate their personal knowledge as much as that provided in textbooks and can develop confidence and personal agency in their learning (Carlson and Erickson 2001; Van Schalkwyk, Chapter 2).

A well-choreographed OBCTL environment provides students with the necessary supportive elements to achieve the outcomes and to demonstrate the processes required to attain those outcomes. These supportive elements involve preparation, performance, interactions with others, completion of various tasks, and continuous assessment of progress and are intended to enable the student to successfully achieve the outcomes of a course or program. The supportive elements are not outcomes. As an example, mastering content, as in *know and understand concepts of the discipline*, can never be

NEW DIRECTIONS FOR TEACHING AND LEARNING, no. 142, Summer 2015 © 2015 Wiley Periodicals, Inc.
Published online in Wiley Online Library (wileyonlinelibrary.com) • DOI: 10.1002/tl.20129

an outcome, since the content alone is inherently inert, empty, and sterile. Rather, outcomes are end results of learning at a specific level, drawing on whatever embedded knowledge and content (i.e., the concepts of the discipline), skills, and supportive processes required for demonstrating achievement of the outcomes. It is a myth to claim that content is not important in OBCTL. One cannot do or demonstrate any skills without basic content knowledge. Students need to learn the facts (i.e., information) and also where to get the facts or information if needed. They also need to learn how to evaluate and question the facts and to discriminate between fact and fallacy. Ultimately, students need to learn how to use the facts, not merely to reproduce them. Thus, in a sound OBCTL environment, students will achieve the outcomes once they embark on employing the supportive elements, learn the basics, and engage with others (the instructor, peers, and the broader context) in an interactive and collaborative manner (Van Offenbeek 2001).

Through the co-construction of personal and public knowledge, strategies emerge that would sustain beyond the realms of the classroom and into the future. Anderson (2002, 1) comments, "Knowledge is fluid and communal, yet personalised. When we share our knowledge with one another, we cannot know what each brings to the sharing. Whatever the outcome, it will be something different than either started with, something socially constructed." Students learn through their collaboration, and the instructor also learns from the students in class, particularly when teaching in a foreign culture. Instruction must therefore allow for learning experiences that go beyond the content, such as the application of rules and procedures, and find creative solutions to problems. Over and above mastering content and skills, students in the OBCTL approach acquire competency to engage in constructive ways with knowledge by devising their own formulas or blueprints to achieve outcomes and apply the knowledge at an even higher level of complexity (Garrison and Archer 2000; Johnson and Johnson 2009; Van der Horst and McDonald 2004).

Thus, in effective OBCTL in an Asian context, the aim is to engage the students—those coming from Confucian heritage culture—among themselves and with the instructor (often a Western-oriented and trained instructor) in different dances or co-actions as they collaboratively reflect on existing knowledge systems, explore different perspectives, and move, for example, from just learning and memorizing theoretical constructs to thinking about the influence of personal experience and to interpreting observations in accordance with relevant theory or empirical work. Therefore, in the planning phase for a course, the first step is to carefully devise and compose intended learning outcomes (ILOs) that will motivate students to exert effort and develop deep learning in their attempt to achieve the critical outcomes for the degree program and the specific outcomes for a course (Van Schalkwyk, Chapter 2). The next step is to engage the students in collaborative skill development through innovative instructional strategies. This requires careful planning and designing the activities and performances of the students both in class and out of class.

Planning for Effective Collaborative Teaching and Learning

In choreographing teaching and learning proactively, the stage emerges for a process of mutual exploration of a variety of topics and resources, and for the establishment of conceptual links and conclusions that are tailored to specific needs that are locally relevant. Students are also given some freedom to co-construct knowledge on the stage of their own lives, often through group work, problem solving, and other ways of applying what they have learned. The instructor who wants to move learning from an input-driven approach involving mostly lectures to an OBCTL approach involving active participation and knowledge co-construction needs knowledge of a variety of instructional strategies to design and plan effective learning in a higher education setting in Asia.

Throughout the process of course design and planning, it is important to keep in mind how the three components of course planning—ILOs, instructional strategies, and assessment techniques—align to facilitate and enhance the teaching and learning environment and ensure that students achieve success (Biggs and Tang 2007). The ILOs for a course include three key components (Van Schalkwyk, Chapter 2):

1. the knowledge component (declarative or functioning);
2. the content or topic; and
3. the performance to be achieved.

The specific learning outcomes for the course articulate the results or performance of narrowly defined aspects of learning required for the course. ILOs also involve supportive elements, such as academic and sociocognitive skills necessary for acquiring the kind of knowledge. Furthermore, the ILOs indicated the topics of interest and levels of understanding required within the course and of the knowledge component. Finally, ILOs express the demonstrations of achievement of the outcomes through participation in a collaborative teaching and learning environment.

Planning a Lesson.   For successful implementation of OBCTL in the classroom, the lesson planning should be aligned with the overall ILOs for the course. Set specific learning outcomes for each lesson, and include the academic and sociocognitive skills necessary for achievement of success and demonstration of attainment of the outcomes. The sociocognitive skills can be taught over the course of the semester or all at once at the beginning of semester. These skills will enable students to perform better individually and in their groups, to gain success in achieving the course and lesson outcomes, and in co-constructing knowledge in their future careers. See more

New Directions for Teaching and Learning • DOI: 10.1002/tl

about sociocognitive skills for learning in the section titled "Sociocognitive Processes for Learning."

Furthermore, for deep learning to occur, students must build their own knowledge through activities that engage them in active learning (Offir, Lev, and Bezalel 2008; Pellegrino and Hilton 2012). Deep learning, as opposed to surface learning, refers to appropriately and meaningfully engaging with learning tasks and elaborating the cognitive activities to handle these tasks. With a deep approach to learning, students reflect, hypothesize, apply, argue, or relate principles to new contexts in response to the teaching environment (Biggs and Tang 2007). Additionally, in most cases, if students have actually constructed their own framework or schema by experimenting, they are more likely to retain the facts and engage in deep learning. The role of the instructor is to facilitate and monitor student learning by providing a framework (i.e., projects of learning and activities) and feedback that enhances students' learning.

Giving Feedback. Monitoring student learning and intervening or providing assistance is important when conducting OBCTL in an Asian context. Asian students do not intuitively know how to perform optimally in a higher education learning context. This is the reason why many students do not participate in class or challenge the instructor and also why many students do not like group work (Phuong-Mai, Terlouw, and Pilot 2005). Therefore, the instructor should systematically observe individual and group activities and collect data through a variety of in-class assessment strategies to determine how each individual and group is performing. When needed, the instructor intervenes to assist students in completing tasks correctly and in working together effectively. Interventions may be needed for task completion or to increase interpersonal and group skills. Although criteria for success can be given beforehand, the students (as a group) can also become involved in designing their own criteria for success. Effective learning happens when students take stock of what they already know and then move beyond it (Angelo and Cross 1993; Barkley, Cross, and Major 2005).

Assigning Learning Activities. The phrase "projects of learning" refers to a variety of tasks and assignments that students engage in to demonstrate that the learning outcomes set for the course and/or lesson have been achieved. Careful planning is necessary for each task that students will participate in, either individually or collaboratively. Whether for in-class activities or for out-of-class assignments, the instructor should integrate the supportive elements and explain these clearly to students, either in writing or verbally. All tasks should also be accompanied with the appropriate criteria according to which students can evaluate their own success in achieving the desired learning. For example, projects such as preparatory reading, writing, and participation activities can all be structured appropriately in order to be within the reach of students. Projects can gradually increase in complexity as students progress.

New Directions for Teaching and Learning • DOI: 10.1002/tl

For in-class activities and tasks, careful planning is necessary to ensure time-on-task efficiency. Based on their time orientation, Asian students often take longer to complete a task than their individualistic counterparts in the West. Therefore, the instructor should be careful to plan projects of learning and in-class activities such that there is sufficient time available to accomplish them. One can avoid the frustration of students taking too long to complete tasks by adopting a flexible attitude and planning carefully to ensure learning takes place. Instead of focusing on covering the content planned for the lesson, one should ensure that effective learning takes place. The Asian student who values effort and who has developed the strategic skills for effective learning and collaboration will be able to acquire additional knowledge outside of the classroom situation.

Classroom Management.   Classroom management forms part of the learning contract and is a consequence of careful planning for a course. A learning contract explicates "what is to be done and how it is proposed to be done and how it is to be assessed" (Biggs and Tang 2007, 220). It is an agreement between the student and the instructor specifying the expected ILOs to be completed during a specific time period and at a certain level of proficiency for a grade. Apart from the ILOs, the learning contract also specifies products and tasks to be completed in class and out of class to demonstrate achievement of the outcomes (i.e., assessment). Furthermore, the learning contract could specify the code of conduct expected of learners during the learning experience.

The *code of conduct* addresses in-class and out-of-class behaviors, ethics, issues regarding plagiarism and noncompliance with conventions of the field or discipline, and any other aspects necessary to ensure the smooth execution of OBCTL (e.g., disability statements, student support systems). Although one can plan carefully to ensure an optimal learning environment, there is always the possibility of learners not complying with expectations and disrupting the processes. For example, learners who are unmotivated for the subject matter might come late or fail to attend class. Absenteeism is a common practice of students who are uninterested in the subject matter. The code of conduct should clearly specify the consequences of such behavior, whether following institutional guidelines (e.g., failure of the course after *n* absences) or establishing one's own measures to deal with such students. It is also helpful to determine students' motivation at the start of a course and to encourage participation by designing interesting in-class and out-of-class activities. When a student seems to be consistently distracted using her or his mobile device in class, I approach this in a positive manner by asking the student, for example, to search for some information on the Internet and report the results to the class. However, it is not helpful when Asian students use their electronic devices to find translations for words because they end up losing track of further discussions and explanations presented by the instructor and/or a peer. Students who are uninterested in the task or assignment may slow down group activities by eliciting off-topic discussions. Group members may not know how to deal with a recalcitrant member. They need advance training in ways of setting up their own contracts when conducting a group assignment and engaging all participants in productive involvement with the task in hand.

In my experience, following the principles of student-centered learning (Chickering and Ehrmann 1996) and appropriately planning for OBCTL prove to be quite effective in avoiding disruptive behavior and in dealing with nonparticipating group members. Instructors who are open and responsive to Asian learners and respect their diverse talents and ways of learning seldom have to deal with difficult behaviors in the classroom. Instructors should integrate diverse strategies for OBCTL and engage students in ways that encourage cooperation, active learning, time on task, and high expectations, and avoid resorting to punitive actions (i.e., negative reinforcement) with which these students are all too familiar.

Essential Supportive Elements for OBCTL

Apart from scanning the vast array of literature on instructional strategies, the rest of this chapter elaborates on the skills and possible projects of learning for in-class and out-of-class assignments in an Asian context. Student-centered, collaborative teaching in the OBCTL model requires thought, energy, and creativity to design and facilitate learning. It also requires the instructor to relinquish the center stage and allow students to collaborate efficiently and effectively in order to achieve the learning outcomes.

Sociocognitive Processes for Learning.   Success in the OBCTL approach involves knowledge of the social and cognitive processes that are supportive of learning and of how to assist Asian students mastering these supportive elements. Although there is wide agreement that the cognitive processes of thinking and learning take place within the individual, collaborative teaching and learning also aim to encourage sociocognitive processes that will assist students to learn through joint activities and in collaboration with their group members (Baxter Magolda 2000). Thus, knowledge and utilization of any or all of a diverse set of strategies provide the instructor with the tools to choreograph a caring and collaborative teaching and learning stage and to assist students in their attempts to co-construct knowledge. For example, knowledge of everyday practices and incorporating tools from the world of work can be quite useful and beneficial in creating a learning context in which students develop and personalize new knowledge systems, attitudes, and skills (Diamond, Koernig, and Iqbal 2008; Van Schalkwyk 2007).

Different sociocognitive processes combine as supportive elements in OBCTL and are important for higher-order thinking and deep learning (Baxter Magolda 2000; Li and Campbell 2008). Research has shown that, regardless of the subject matter, students who *work in groups achieve better results* and are more satisfied with their learning experience (Trotter and Roberts 2006). The specific skills that constitute effective learning involve interactions such as communication, analytical thinking, integration of ideas, and reasoning. These skills are not unique to the social context of collaborative learning and can be accomplished by individual students alone. However, when deployed in collaborative and interactive settings and when promoting higher-level cognitive processes through active learning within the group, deep learning occurs that goes beyond memorization and comprehension.

Individual Participation.   King (2007) proposes a set of activities that promote higher-level cognitive processes and states that the instructor has to choreograph activities to elicit and regulate these specific learning processes. In the following section, the focus is on exploring activities for higher-level learning and the implications of these activities for individual participation in an OBCTL environment in an Asian context. Group processes are discussed under the subheading "Successful Group Work."

Although the sociocognitive processes to be discussed might be common among non-Asian students, they do not come naturally to Asian students trained in traditional educational systems. However, in order to develop these processes in higher education settings, where the learning outcomes include both discipline-specific knowledge and social skills and attitudes, it is necessary to choreograph in-class activities carefully and engage students actively. Effectively structuring, prompting, and facilitating these processes along with the skills necessary to generate deep learning should be the primary objective when preparing in-class and out-of-class tasks for an OBCTL setting.

Thinking Aloud.   Language is a way in which to "think aloud" and construct meaning in an interactive manner. According to King (2007, 19), "Talking or writing about the task at hand...makes thinking explicit and available" and provides a space to clarify concepts and ideas, elaborate on them, evaluate existing knowledge, and reconceptualize ideas into new knowledge maps. However, when Asian students have to speak in a nonnative language (e.g., English), the social act of talking and negotiating can be lost when students feel they are not sufficiently competent in the language of tuition and find it difficult to speak with their foreign instructors (Shi 2006; Trotter and Roberts 2006). They tend to speak softly—particularly to the instructor, whom they respect for her or his language proficiency—to avoid being heard using incorrect pronunciation or making errors with grammar. When asked to repeat, the fear of being ridiculed or of being less than perfect make them speak even more quietly. Therefore, the instructor should make every effort to encourage verbal communication in the language of instruction (e.g., English) and build students' confidence by training them in the process of *thinking aloud*. It is helpful to talk slowly and pronounce clearly, provide lecture outlines prior to class and written feedback using proper language (no abbreviations or colloquialisms), and accept that the language barrier is not an excuse for lack of participation (i.e., thinking aloud).

Explaining. The focus in OBCTL is for students to be able to explain concepts to others so that they will understand. While using one's own words, the challenge is to be effective in different modes of communication (verbally and in writing). Providing "a useful explanation requires analytical thinking, as the explainer must make connections between the phenomenon being explained and prior knowledge" (King 2007, 20). Such explanations should be in the student's own words, not a mere repetition of memorized material—a form of plagiarism that should be discouraged. Although Asian students often assume that memorizing and regurgitating the material are a form of respect for the originator of ideas, they have to develop the skill to express ideas and give examples in their own words. Nonetheless, students who explain the material in the nonnative language (e.g., English) to fellow group members help with the expansion of vocabulary and spontaneous verbal communication necessary for participating in the learning process and knowledge co-construction (Shi 2006). However, Asian students have to be continuously encouraged to verbalize and communicate in their own words in order to build confidence and ensure successful participation in collaborative knowledge co-construction. They can also be encouraged to send their questions and explanations via email or through discussion forums using the technologies available. The instructor should respond to such email correspondence and forums within twenty-four hours and follow up in class.

Asking Thought-Provoking Questions. Few people know instinctively how to ask thought-provoking questions—it is a learned art and calls for higher-level cognitive processes (King 2007). Learning how to ask thought-provoking questions is a valuable learning activity within OBCTL and encourages students to share experiences and understanding of course materials during group discussions in class. Asian students, who were taught not to question the wisdom of their teacher or the textbook, in particular need guidance in learning how to ask questions and the different kinds of questions that should be asked in a learning context. Students can learn to do this by the instructor and other students asking questions related to a written paragraph or letting students develop a set of questions prior to class for use as an in-class quiz based on the prescribed reading.

Elaborating. Mental representations are reorganized and increased in complexity when elaboration of an issue, topic, or idea takes place by giving examples, generating metaphors, and relating new material to what is already known. When asked to elaborate, Asian students may hesitate because they lack confidence in their personal knowledge. Coming from a culture where adding and opposing is considered inappropriate in the presence of the out group (i.e., the instructor and other students), Asian students need to gain confidence in their own viewpoints and ideas about the topic. The instructor should facilitate the processes of explaining,

NEW DIRECTIONS FOR TEACHING AND LEARNING • DOI: 10.1002/tl

questioning, and elaborating, and encourage students to trust and respect their own voices.

Argumentation.   Similar to elaboration, argumentation is a way of analyzing a topic and arriving at a deeper level of understanding. Argumentation is integral to effective co-construction of meaning and offers opportunities to explore existing knowledge, negotiate and reconceptualize meanings, justify viewpoints, and integrate these with new ideas to reach deeper understanding about the topic under discussion (King 2007). However, the concept of argumentation is, in many ways, alien to Confucian heritage culture students. Trained from early on to perceive argumentation as conflict inducing, Asian students tend to avoid arguments and seek harmony through compromise or conformity. Thus, in an Asian context, students have to learn the meaning and appropriateness of argumentation and rhetoric along with the art of developing sound arguments and detecting faulty ones. They also have to learn how to employ argumentation within group discussions without offending their cultural heritage or creating conflict. Argumentation, when appropriately choreographed in OBCTL, can aid students in developing critical thinking and promote deep learning.

Reconciling Cognitive Discrepancies.   Disagreements, cognitive discrepancies, and even conflict are unavoidable in OBCTL. However, constructive conflict—the process of recognizing conceptual discrepancies and negotiating new meanings—is an integral part of deep learning (Baxter Magolda 2000). As with argumentation, Asian students tend to avoid conflict and withdraw from conversations that elicit cognitive discrepancies. Rather than clearly articulating their own positions, explaining their ideas, defending their views, and verbalizing confusions, they tend to evade conflict by conforming or compromising. It is therefore necessary to carefully choreograph and teach skills for recognizing misconceptions, acknowledging gaps in knowledge, presenting thoughts, and in a reasoned manner dealing with cognitive discrepancies.

Modeling of Cognition.   Social modeling has long been accepted as a form of learning that encourages cognition and metacognition (King 2007). In OBCTL, the instructor should create a context in which skilled peers demonstrate the use of explaining, questioning, and elaborating. Instead of modeling only on the instructor, as is the tradition in Asian education systems, peer modeling becomes a powerful way of learning during interaction. Thus, through thinking aloud, effective prompting (questioning), and sharing ideas in a constructive and negotiated manner, students can participate in higher-level cognitive modeling.

Successful Group Work.   All successful collaborative learning involves effective group functioning. In this section, I identify and explicate the supportive elements of how to conduct group work and enhance deep learning in the OBCTL approach. There is an abundance of literature on the topic of the development of collaborative learning in Western education systems (e.g., Anderson 2002; Johnson and Johnson 1999; Napier and

Gershenfeld 2004; Pellegrino and Hilton 2012; Richlin 2006). In the Asian context, collaborative learning has been applied mostly for second-language instruction, but there are also examples of collaborative learning in multicultural settings, such as Australia, New Zealand, and Britain (e.g., Baker and Clark 2010; Li and Campbell 2008). Nonetheless, very little (if any) literature prevails about the implementation of collaborative teaching and learning in a more homogeneous educational setting such as universities in Asia. By integrating the literature on culturally appropriate and responsive pedagogy (Biggs 2003; Phuong-Mai, Terlouw, and Pilot 2005) with that of OBCTL, I hope to identify the supportive elements essential for planning high-quality deep learning experiences in Asian higher education contexts.

Gergen (2009) holds the view that knowledge and understanding are relational achievements and the aim of education should be the facilitation of relational processes or patterns of interaction that promote successful learning outcomes. Relational pedagogy, with its focus on the student's circles of participation (Gergen 2009), and social interdependence theory (Johnson and Johnson 2009) provide insights into the importance of considering different relational circles to explore a variety of innovative practices for OBCTL. Building on the principles of systems theory and reciprocal determinism, relational pedagogy and social interdependence theory consider the group as a dynamic whole where change in any one member facilitates change within the entire group. Group members are therefore interdependent through common goals, and a state of tension arises that motivates movement toward the accomplishment of goals.

Johnson and Johnson (2009) identify three types of groups that can be employed in a classroom. *Informal learning groups* are temporary groups of students that form during a single class session and meet a specific purpose (e.g., discuss before reporting out to the larger class). *Formal learning groups* are out-of-class teams coming together to complete a specific, time-limited task (e.g., producing a semester-long project or a task that can be completed in one class period). *Base groups*, study teams, or learning communities are often long-term groups whose membership may be self-selected. Such groups may study together for class tests or exams and may work together for a whole semester or longer. Whether students are collaborating to achieve a shared learning goal and complete jointly a task or assignment (formal collaboration), temporarily working together to achieve a joint learning goal (informal collaboration), or engaging in a long-term collaborative learning group (collaborating base group), the instructor needs to plan a variety of activities and projects that will enhance students' sociocognitive skill development and ensure success within the OBCTL model.

Five key elements characterize effective collaboration within the highly competitive environment of tertiary education (Johnson and Johnson 2009). Although these elements are universal for all students in a collaborative teaching and learning environment, they are explored here for developing culturally appropriate/responsive application within a higher education context comprising predominantly Asian students. These five elements are

1. positive interdependence;
2. individual accountability;
3. constructive interaction;
4. social skills; and
5. group processes.

Positive Interdependence.   The term "positive interdependence" refers to the positive correlation between attaining group goals and cooperating in order for everyone to attain their individual goals (Johnson and Johnson 2009). Alternatively, the term "negative interdependence" refers to individuals who are competitively linked failing to obtain group goals, or when individuals perceive the achievement of their goals as unrelated to the goal achievement of others. Establishing positive interdependence in multicultural groups comprising a mix of Asian students or of an Asian-Western student mix is more challenging than for homogeneous groups (i.e., predominantly Chinese or Japanese students). Even in a monocultural group, students have difficulty seeing the advantages of working with others to achieve educational goals.

Although interdependence is not an unfamiliar concept in Asian cultures (Li and Campbell 2008), working together in an interdependent manner is interpreted somewhat differently. For example, in the family and community, interdependence is usually aimed at economic goals and social harmony. However, in an educational setting, Asian students perceive academic achievement as an individual goal and have difficulty forming close interpersonal bonds within the group, particularly if the group is composed of multicultural students (Campbell and Li 2007). Asian students, like their non-Asian counterparts, are also competitive and want to be recognized for their individual performance (Li and Campbell 2008; Soosay 2009). Nonetheless, it is widely acknowledged the individuals achieve more with positive goal interdependence than when they work individually or competitively. Johnson and Johnson (2009) identify three areas of positive interdependence: outcome, means, and boundary interdependence. Group members who agree on the expected outcome they want to achieve develop positive interdependence and will share resources, roles, and tasks equally when the boundaries are clearly defined, ensuring that each member knows who is interdependent with whom and bound together throughout the group process.

Individual Accountability.   Whereas positive interdependence binds group members together, it is also necessary to develop a sense of individual accountability and personal responsibility in order to successfully complete one's share of the work and to facilitate the work of other group members (Johnson and Johnson 2009). Individual accountability is important for group success. Giving feedback where group members compare their performance against a standard and where individual members are assessed for their performance increases motivation and minimizes social loafing (Johnson and Johnson, 2009). Asian students who experience a lack of individual accountability and perceive that the contributions of each member are not equally valued tend to exhibit reduced personal responsibility and group cohesiveness. Social loafing becomes more prevalent and hampers positive interdependence, and groups become nonfunctional. Furthermore, establishing clear mechanisms for individual accountability enables Asian students to achieve personal success while simultaneously motivating them to contribute toward group goals. When they know their individual contributions will improve group performance and help them achieve individual success, they are more willing to participate in the group and engage in constructive interactions.

Constructive Interaction.   When group members encourage and facilitate each other's efforts to accomplish the group's goals, group work also becomes meaningful to the Asian student. That is, individual behavior should lead to trustworthiness, efficient and effective exchange of resources and information, helping and assisting when needed, striving for mutual benefits, achieving mutual goals, exerting sufficient levels of effort with low anxiety and stress, influencing and challenging each other, providing feedback, and accurately taking the perspective of others. Contrary to constructive interaction, "*oppositional interaction* occurs as individuals discourage, block, and obstruct each other's efforts to achieve their goals" (Johnson and Johnson 2009, 369). Of course, there is no interaction when individuals work independently. The instructor should include opportunities to develop constructive interaction skills in both the individual and the group. Perceiving their behaviors within the group as personally beneficial and to the advantage of the group stimulates Asian students to collaborate more positively, leading to constructive instead of oppositional interaction. It is, however, important to note that constructive interaction does not imply blindly conforming to group beliefs. Rather, as with students elsewhere, Asian students need to develop supportive elements for individual accountability and collaborate effectively within the group.

Social Skills.   Baxter Magolda (2000) elaborates on the complex intrapersonal, interpersonal, and cognitive skills levels necessary for effective collaboration in groups and to promote holistic learning and development. Interpersonal and small-group skills do not come automatically or naturally to most students and even less so to Asian students. To collaborate effectively and achieve learning outcomes, group members must get to know and trust each other. Doing this takes time when students are assigned to groups having members with whom they are not familiar (e.g., friends). In the group, students have to communicate accurately and unambiguously using the skills indicated as supportive elements for individual participation. They also have to accept and support each other, developing positive interdependence and constructive interaction during in-class activities. Finally, social skills in higher education settings imply that students develop the ability to resolve conflicts constructively, to set standards for individual and group achievement, and to engage the group in establishing a clear contract for task performance.

Group members should engage in co-constructive meaning making (Chapman, Ramondt, and Smiley 2005; Suthers and Hundhausen 2003) and develop skills that will promote the highest achievement and productivity in an OBCTL setting. These skills are often absent due to the competitive nature of previous schooling. Therefore, appropriately choreographed OBCTL should include training in interpersonal skills. When Asian students are taught the necessary social skills and given feedback as to how they engaged in the social skills, their relationships become more positive, and both group success and individual success are enhanced.

Group Processes.   In group work, it is often difficult to attain satisfactory learning when group processes are not appropriately clarified and group members are unclear about the tasks necessary to achieve group goals (Johnson and Johnson 2009). Therefore, when including group work in OBCTL, either the instructor or the group has to set standards for reflecting on individual actions that are helpful and to promote decisions among group members regarding the actions that need to be changed or can continue for the group to function properly. While there is no real difference in how Asian and non-Asian students engage in group processes, in an Asian context the instructor should include checkpoints for students to regularly clarify the group's goals, increase members' awareness of the resources available to them, and strengthen involvement in the group's efforts. This is usually done through classroom assessment techniques and regular self- and peer evaluations of group processes (Angelo and Cross 1993).

In many Asian higher education contexts, the students are first-generation university students with little or no frame of reference for how to engage in higher education learning goals and even less for collaborative learning and group work. Thus, it is helpful to build up each group member's confidence and to enhance his or her self-esteem in order to increase commitment to group ideals and improve positive interdependence. On one hand, each group member should recognize and believe in the value of his or her contributions within the group. Members also have to express their respect toward the group and each member within the group. Students need to develop an awareness of how their personal contributions help the group as a whole to succeed as well as themselves to achieve deep learning. For this to happen, the instructor should incorporate the necessary mechanisms for developing the group processes that will help students achieve effective learning in an OBCTL environment.

Strategies for Projects of Learning in OBCTL

Since the inception of OBCTL in educational settings some forty years ago—both at school level and in tertiary education settings—a vast repertoire of research has ensued providing evidence and strong support for the effectiveness of well-choreographed collaborative teaching and learning (e.g., see Angelo and Cross 1993; Barkley, Cross, and Major 2005; Baxter Magolda 2000; Doyle 2008; Millis and Cottell 1998; Richlin 2006). In this section, the focus is on some in-class and out-of-class strategies and activities that can help the Western-oriented instructor plan and design effective collaborative teaching and learning. The next section focuses on planning for in-class and out-of-class activities and interactions within the OBCTL model and when implementing these within an Asian higher education context.

Preclass Activities.   Instructors are often concerned that the facilitation of group activities will prevent them from covering the content prescribed for the course. Asian students who have grown up in a more passive learning environment also expect the instructor to present extensive lectures on the topic. These students then prepare for examinations by memorizing lecture notes provided by the instructor. This approach relates more to information transference than to constructing useful knowledge for future application. In the OBCTL approach, the content per se is not the prime focus of learning. Rather, the focus is on how the students can access the content and other information—often contained in textbooks (and the lecture) but also available in a variety of other resources, such as the library, scholarly articles, and the Internet. Students need to demonstrate their ability to use the content to co-construct new and personalized knowledge, solve real-life problems, and achieve the ILOs. Thus, learning takes place when the students develop skills that will equip them for lifelong learning and active participation in their future careers.

Various individual and group activities can be structured to cover the content while simultaneously acquiring the skills for accessing and constructing new knowledge. Preclass assignments are one way of getting students involved with the content in the textbook or other resources and to come to class prepared to work with the material at higher cognitive levels and in collaboration with their peers. These preclass assignments allow the instructor to plan for the best use of limited classroom time and ensure that students come to class with a readiness and interest in the topic, leading to active group participation and deep learning. Thus, the course is designed with both in-class and out-of-class activities to cover the content and to facilitate active engagement with the course materials (see Figure 3.1).

Preclass assignments involve reading (e.g., sections in the textbook or scholarly articles), writing, or devising questions on the topic to be discussed during the next lesson. These assignments should be structured such that they support development of the sociocognitive skills implied in the ILOs for the course. For example, if the ILO states that the student should

Figure 3.1. Designing Out-of-Class and In-Class Assignments to Cover Content and Ensure Deep Learning

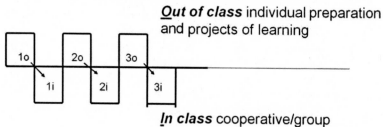

be able to *analyze* and *critique* a topic of interest (e.g., a section in the textbook), the reading should be aimed at developing the skills for analysis and critique. These skills can be transferred to other contexts even when the topic changes. Instructors should structure preclass (and other) activities in such a manner that they can integrate the preparation as an in-class activity, engage the students in demonstrating achievement of ILOs, and gain feedback of areas that still need further elaboration or teaching. Some preclass activities can also be structured to involve a group of students as a learning community.

Following the preclass assignments and as with other ILOs, instructors need to obtain evidence that the task has been achieved by following up the preparation with an evaluation process. Demonstration of achievement of ILOs could involve a quiz specifically designed to assess the outcomes envisioned for the preparation task, a brief verbal presentation or summary of key points in the reading, time set aside to discuss the topic in a small group, or a peer assessment where students question one another on the topic. There are many possible activities aimed at providing students with an opportunity to demonstrate in class their preparation for and achievement of the expected ILOs (e.g., see Barkley, Cross, and Major 2005). Here are some examples.

Lesson Prep.   The *lesson prep* is a useful preclass assignment and can assist instructors in checking, for example, attendance. That is, students prepare for the next class by reading the prescribed sections and preparing critical thinking questions to submit as an "entry ticket" to the class. A quick overview of the students' questions as they enter and submit can then be used, during the first ten minutes or so, to stimulate further discussion on the topic for the lesson and to help students develop the art of questioning. The lesson prep is also useful in guiding instructors toward making adjustments to future lesson plans to ensure that teaching leads to learning and the achievement of the ILOs. Asking students to add a paragraph about what they have learned at the end of the lesson provides useful evidence of whether the instruction has been successful.

Purposeful Reading.   The task of *purposeful reading* is specifically designed to encourage the development of sociocognitive skills embedded in the ILOs and has great use for the (impromptu) structuring of in-class group discussions as well as stimulating further exploration of the topic. Students have to respond to predesigned, open-ended questions about the reading—for example, "What argument(s) is the author making?," "What assumptions are evident in the paper?," and "What inferences did the author make based on the data?" The responses can also be used to evaluate or assess their achievement of the ILOs, for generating model answers based on a group discussion of their respective responses to the prepared reading, and for adjustment of future lesson plans.

In-Class Collaborative Learning Activities.   Group activities in the OBCTL approach highlight individual group members' (the students') abilities and contributions as well as group participation and collaboration. Students need to acquire skills to share authority and accept responsibility within a team framework, and in-class activities should be structured in a learner-centered rather than teacher-centered manner. Through developing sociocognitive skills in the group activities, students become acquainted with the collaborative processes that can be applied in different settings beyond the classroom. However, OBCTL is not as controllable as a teacher-centered and lecture setting. It is also not an unstructured discussion or a shortcut to faculty preparation time. Rather, careful planning of group activities is important and will result in deep learning (Biggs and Tang 2007; Chapman, Ramondt, and Smiley 2005; Diamond, Koernig, and Iqbal 2008). The group activities and products (i.e., results of collaboration) should relate to the content of the course and the supportive elements of OBCTL for the achievement of the ILOs. These activities should involve students in sustained intensive work, both independently and interdependently, and help students learn the technologies of the discipline or field. The instructor shifts from dispensing information to designing and managing the instructional process.

Managing Group Activities.   When planning for group activities, it is necessary to organize students at the start of the class or semester. Most students tend to sit with their friends or those whom they already know. However, this is not reflective of the real world of work where people usually work with those with whom they are not familiar at the outset—though people do befriend coworkers after a while. In the OBCTL approach, group formation is often instructor selected rather than randomly or student selected. That is, the instructor organizes groups in any way that suits the overall outcomes for the course. Groups can also be organized for in-class discussion at the start of each lesson followed by reassignment of students to different groups before starting the group discussion. Alternatively, groups can be formed at the start of the semester to function as a whole for both in-class discussions and out-of-class assignments or projects.

There are various methods for assigning students to groups (e.g., see Barkley, Cross, and Major 2005; Millis 2002). Irrespective of which particular method instructors choose for assigning students to groups, they should keep the following points in mind, particularly when working in an Asian higher education setting:

- *Group size matters.* Groups ranging in size from pairs (i.e., two students) to seven students are manageable and allow group members to participate equally. If the group is too large, social loafing or freeloading or even conforming is an option for the lazy, uninterested, or shy student; if the group is too small, each student might experience role overload and have difficulty achieving the goals. Knowing the size of groups helps with preparing the materials needed to facilitate in-class discussion and in arranging the classroom in an effective manner. Small groups also work more easily when the classroom is set up with fixed seats—four to five students sitting in two rows can easily turn around to face one another for the discussion, while large-group activities are more difficult to manage in such a setting.
- *Create a learning community.* Groups should remain together long enough to establish positive working relationships and develop team-building skills (formal learning groups). For example, at the start of the semester, instructors can assign a number from 1 to 7 (or use playing cards, colors, or symbols) to students as they enter the classroom. Students then sit with those having the same number, card, color, or symbol, forming small groups. Instructors can also determine students' self-defined attributes—written on an index card at the start of the semester—and group stronger students with weaker students.
- *Appoint a leader.* Asian students coming from a Confucian heritage culture perceive a well-functioning learning community as one with unequal relationships and clear leadership (Phuong-Mai, Terlouw, and Pilot 2005). Thus, instructors should consider assigning a group leader who can change every time the group functions in class.
- *Role appropriation.* Well-defined roles within the group and alternating these roles from time to time give each student an opportunity to develop the skills associated with the role. Each student should also be assigned a role for the duration of the lesson. For example, during in-class discussions, the instructor calls on the "recorder" to take notes and record ideas and decisions, the "presenter" to share teamwork or ideas with other teams in the class, the "participation checker" to keep track of each group member's participation, and the "leader" to ensure that everyone participates and to check for understanding and learning. Note that Asian students do not necessarily have the skills required for their role. This could be an opportunity to develop various competencies relevant to the world of work. The assigned roles must also be aligned with the ILOs for the course—that is, an ILO stating, for example, *summarize*

the principles requires note-taking skills and the ability to conceptualize a response. The recorder and the presenter will each develop these skills while acting on their assigned roles in the group discussion.

Planning and Facilitating Groups.   Planning and facilitating group activities in the OBCTL approach require careful consideration. Barkley, Cross, and Major (2005) propose that planning and facilitating group activities in OBCTL involve five different stages:

1. *Before.* Decide on how to form groups and how many students per group. Plan activities to align with the ILOs for the course, gather adequate materials, estimate the amount of time on task (i.e., time students will take to complete the task), and prepare extension activities to keep groups who finish early occupied.
2. *Beginning.* Explain the objective of the activity, and tell the students how the groups will operate. Asian students work best in groups when tasks are clearly defined, expectations for collaboration specified, and assessment criteria for groups and individual accountability are appropriately outlined at the start of the lesson or activity.
3. *During.* Check in with groups to monitor their process and progress and help nonfunctioning groups to learn how to solve problems and become productive. Allow sufficient time for discussion—communicating in one's nonnative language often takes longer, and Asian students, with their embedded time orientation, their need to save face, and their search for structure, in particular need more time to get started.
4. *Ending.* Structure closure activities for groups to present findings to the class and contribute to a bigger learning outcome. Provide structured opportunities for air time in which students can debate, summarize, and synthesize their group discussion.
5. *After.* Incorporate a "reflection" stage for students to analyze what they have learned, identify strengths and weaknesses of the learning process, and propose adaptations. Give feedback on process and content of discussions, and incorporate self- and peer evaluation that will enable students to evaluate their own learning and make adaptations for the future. Asian students, with their capacity for effort and deep learning, want to know what they have to do to be more effective and achieve success in the academic environment.

As noted before, there are numerous resources to guide OBCTL instructors in designing in-class and out-of-class collaborative activities. Instructors should decide on a mix of activities to shape basic skills and procedures, present information, guide inquiry, monitor individual and group activities, and support the achievement of the ILOs for the course. They should balance the need for support with using class time effectively—some skills for collaborative learning need to be taught, while others need to be practiced through repetitive actions. The next examples are specifically adapted to fit the teaching of Asian students.

The Art of Questioning.   Because the power hierarchy does not encourage Asian students to ask questions of the instructor or challenge superiors, they often do not know how to ask questions, even of one another. However, developing critical thinking as proposed in the ILOs demands the art of questioning. Instructors should consider asking students to write questions anonymously on sticky notes. The students can post these on a designated surface, and instructors can pick up the questions to focus the discussion of the topic. Students can also participate in organizing the questions according to themes related to the topic under discussion. Developing the art of questioning has positive implications for group discussions exploring course content and for acquiring essential skills to achieve success in a higher-education learning environment.

As a classroom activity first involving the whole class and then facilitating small-group discussions, instructors can ask students to write on the classroom whiteboard a question they have prepared from their assigned reading. Instructors can facilitate an open discussion of the question with the whole class identifying the type of question and the response each type of question could elicit. Then instructors can assign small groups to analyze the questions that each group member has prepared from the reading and facilitate the development of model answers. Instructors can remind students of the different types of questions—factual, conceptual, and normative questions and possible combinations of such questions—and give some examples from their discipline. They can also engage students with knowledge, application, and synthesizing questions that represent different levels of cognitive engagement. Again, instructors should give examples from their discipline and facilitate the development of model answers based on the type of question asked.

In-Class Small-Group Discussion.   In-class small-group discussions are a good way of engaging Asian students and encouraging the development of the supportive elements of listening, thinking aloud, elaborating and explaining, asking thought-provoking questions, and argumentation. In small groups with their peers (rather than with the instructor), Asian students are willing to demonstrate their knowledge and are free to challenge the expert knowledge of other sources (e.g., the textbook). Once they have participated in a small-group discussion and tested their ideas, Asian students are also more willing to communicate responses in the large group and to the instructor. Instructors can use the small-group discussion in a variety of ways to stimulate further exploration of the course content or topic, engage students in group processes, and identify areas in which knowledge is still limited, thus necessitating adjustment of the lesson plan. Small-group discussions may also be used to assess students' demonstration of achievement of the ILOs.

Examples of discipline-specific applications for these small-group activities:

- *English composition.* What makes a written argument effective?
- *Introduction to anthropology* (or any subject). Post three questions online for pairs to prepare for the in-class activity. During the class, they meet as two-person groups to discuss, compare, and contrast their responses before submitting a group worksheet.
- *Introduction to music.* What musician recording today (from any style) do you think people will still be listening to fifty years from now, and why?
- *Calculus.* What homework problem did you find most difficult, and why?
- *Business management.* How has the current business environment been affected by managerial accounting?
- *Other.*
  - What one idea have you heard in the lesson that you would like to remember and adapt for use in your personal life?
  - What are the most important qualities of an effective leader?
  - What are some ethical or societal issues related to gene modification?
  - How should health care professionals respond when asked to perform procedures they find morally objectionable?

In large classes, multiple small groups can participate in structured in-class activities by assigning specific tasks or preparation for the class. In the activity "*send a problem*" (see Barkley, Cross, and Major 2005), small groups of students (four or more members) can work on a task that then gets sent on to the next group for evaluation and thus involves all students in a large class in the learning activity. For example, students in the small group will try to solve a problem and pass the problem and their solution to the next small group, which does the same, while the final group evaluates the two solutions for their efficacy. This activity helps students practice thinking skills for effective problem solving and for comparing and discriminating among solutions. Different problems related to the lesson topic can be given to the small groups, which simultaneously work on the solution. Two discipline specific examples suffice to illustrate the use of "*send a problem*" in a single lesson or across different lessons. In an urban planning course, students have to find solutions to a residential rezoning problem. In an English literature course, students are divided into three online forums in the first week of class to each explore solutions to a problem relating a text to a historical context. During the second week, solutions are passed on to another small group during an in-class activity, while the third week is an open access week for all groups to evaluate the responses of each group (either in-class or online).

Further examples of specific applications for small-group discussion activities include:

- *Introduction to art.* Ask students to develop two or three questions about each of the major schools of art. Questions must address defining features and be thought provoking.
- *Human anatomy and physiology* (or any subject). Ask students to develop two or three multiple-choice questions with four response options (correct one indicated), and conduct in-class learning cells where students question a partner and explain the rationale for the correct response. This activity encourages students to listen actively and focus on the content.
- *Social psychology.* Individual students keep a log for one week of prejudiced comments overheard in their daily lives. In class, all students participate in a pretest on effective responses to prejudiced comments, role-play scenarios based on their logs, and engage in a posttest to check for changes in their responses.

Another interesting group activity for in-class application is the *jigsaw with concept mapping.* Students will develop knowledge about a given theme or area and then teach it to others. This activity motivates students to prepare for the lesson, learn and process information more deeply, and co-construct knowledge for problem solving. Provide each student in the home-group with a different subtopic or area related to the overall theme for the lesson and their preparation for class—that is, in each home-group, one student is assigned subtopic 1, another subtopic 2, and so on. Each student individually creates a concept map of her or his knowledge and understanding of the topic. All students with subtopic 1 gather together (i.e., regrouping for the duration of the activity) to create a combined concept map for their subtopic, as do students assigned the other subtopics. The subtopic groups post their concept map on the classroom wall, and one student remains with the map to explain the content. Other students circulate so that each student will learn about a different subtopic related to the theme from the concept maps posted on the wall. Then students gather with their original home-group members to create an overview concept map of the theme for the lesson that combines all the learning from different posted concept maps. The activity can be conducted over several lessons, allowing students time to generate copies for the four to six subtopic concept maps for distribution to the original home-groups during the last phase of the activity. Combined concept maps can also be posted online for all students to access and learn from one another.

Conclusion

Careful planning and integration of the supportive elements for individual participation and group work in the preclass, in-class, and out-of-class activities are essential for successful implementation of OBCTL in an Asian higher education setting. Postdesign revision is also necessary. Regular reflection on one's own performance helps instructors to make changes when necessary and to ensure the objectives for teaching excellence are met. It is also helpful for instructors to collaborate with colleagues to form an instructor learning community or to engage in professional development groups to share ideas and resolve frustrations. For example, instructors can use a Teaching Goals Inventory (Angelo and Cross 1993) as framework for self-assessment and for discussion in the instructor learning community. The purpose of inventories for self- or peer evaluation is to help instructors become aware of what they want to accomplish in a course, help with locating and adapting techniques they can use to assess how well they are achieving their teaching and learning goals, and provide a starting point for discussion of teaching and learning goals among colleagues. Success in choreographing the stage for OBCTL requires regular evaluation of one's own performance and a willingness to make changes when necessary.

References

Anderson, H. 2002. "Supervision as a Collaborative Learning Community." *Music Therapy Today*. http://www.wfmt.info/Musictherapyworld/startup/MTT2000-3.pdf.

Angelo, T. A., and K. P. Cross. 1993. *Classroom Assessment Techniques—A Handbook for College Teachers*, 2nd ed. San Francisco, CA: Jossey-Bass.

Baker, T., and J. Clark. 2010. "Cooperative Learning—A Double-Edged Sword: A Cooperative Learning Model for Use with Diverse Student Groups." *International Education* 21: 257–268.

Barkley, E. F., K. P. Cross, and C. H. Major. 2005. *Collaborative Learning Techniques: A Handbook for College Faculty*. San Francisco, CA: Jossey-Bass.

Baxter Magolda, M. 2000. "Teaching to Promote Holistic Learning and Development." In *Teaching to Promote Intellectual and Personal Maturity: Incorporating Students' Worldviews and Identities into the Learning Process*, New Directions for Teaching and Learning, no. 82, edited by M. Baxter Magolda, 88–98. San Francisco, CA: Jossey-Bass.

Biggs, J., ed. 2003. *Teaching for Quality Learning at University*, 2nd ed. Maidenhead, UK: Open University Press.

Biggs, J., and C. Tang. 2007. *Teaching for Quality Learning at University: What the Student Does*, 3rd ed. Berkshire, UK: SRHE and Open University Press.

Campbell, J., and M. Li. 2007. "Asian Students' Voices: An Empirical Study of Asian Students' Learning Experiences at a New Zealand University." *Journal of Studies in International Education* 12: 375–396.

Carlson, T. D., and M. J. Erickson. 2001. "Honoring and Privileging Personal Experience and Knowledge: Ideas for a Narrative Therapy Approach to the Training and Supervision of New Therapists." *Contemporary Family Therapy* 23: 199–220.

Chapman, C., L. Ramondt, and G. Smiley. 2005. "Strong Community, Deep Learning: Exploring the Link." *Innovations in Education and Teaching International* 42: 217–230.

Chickering, A. W., and S. C. Ehrmann. 1996. "Implementing the Seven Principles." *AAHEBulletin.com.* http://sphweb.bumc.bu.edu/otlt/teachingLibrary/Technology /seven_principles.pdf.

Diamond, N., S. K. Koernig, and Z. Iqbal. 2008. "Uniting Active and Deep Learning to Teach Problem-Solving Skills: Strategic Tools and the Learning Spiral." *Journal of Marketing Education* 30: 116–129.

Doyle, T. 2008. *Helping Students Learn in a Learner-Centered Environment: A Guide to Teaching Higher Education.* Sterling, VA: Stylus.

Garrison, D. R., and W. Archer. 2000. *A Transactional Perspective on Teaching and Learning: A Framework for Adult and Higher Education.* Amsterdam, the Netherlands: Pergamon Press.

Gergen, K. J. 2009. *Relational Being: Beyond Self and Community.* New York, NY: Oxford University Press.

Johnson, D. W., and R. T. Johnson. 1999. *Learning Together and Alone: Cooperative, Competitive, and Individualistic Learning,* 5th ed. Upper Saddle River, NJ: Merrill.

Johnson, D. W., and R. T. Johnson. 2009. "An Educational Psychology Success Story: Social Interdependence Theory and Cooperative Learning." *Educational Researchers* 38: 365–379.

King, A. 2007. "Scripting Collaborative Learning Processes: A Cognitive Perspective." In *Scripting Computer-Supported Collaborative Learning,* Vol. 6, edited by F. Fisher, I. Kollar, H. Mandl, and J. M. Haake, 13–37. New York, NY: Springer.

Li, M., and J. Campbell. 2008. "Asian Students' Perceptions of Group Work and Group Assignments in a New Zealand Tertiary Institution." *Intercultural Education* 19: 203–216.

Millis, B. J. 2002. "Enhancing Learning—and More—through Cooperative Learning." *IDEA Paper 38.* http://ideaedu.org/sites/default/files/IDEA_Paper_38.pdf.

Millis, B. J., and P. C. Cottell, Jr., eds. 1998. *Cooperative Learning for Higher Education Faculty.* Phoenix, AZ: Oryx Press.

Napier, R. W., and M. K. Gershenfeld. 2004. *Groups: Theory and Experience.* Boston, MA: Houghton Mifflin.

Offir, B., Y. Lev, and R. Bezalel. 2008. "Surface and Deep Learning Processes in Distance Education: Synchronous versus Asynchronous Systems." *Computers and Education* 51: 1172–1183.

Pellegrino, J. W., and M. L. Hilton, eds. 2012. *Education for Life and Work: Developing Transferable Knowledge and Skills in the 21st Century.* Washington, DC: National Academies Press.

Phuong-Mai, N., C. Terlouw, and A. Pilot. 2005. "Cooperative Learning vs. Confucian Heritage Culture's Collectivism: Confrontation to Reveal Some Cultural Conflicts and Mismatch." *Asia Europe Journal* 3: 403–419.

Richlin, L. 2006. *Blueprint for Learning—Constructing College Courses to Facilitate, Assess, and Document Learning.* Sterling, VA: Stylus.

Shi, L. 2006. "The Successors to Confucianism or a New Generation? A Questionnaire Study on Chinese Students' Culture of Learning English." *Language, Culture and Curriculum* 19: 122–147.

Soosay, C. 2009. "International and Domestic Students' Perspectives on Teaching and Learning." *Journal of International Education in Business* 2: 20–32.

Suthers, D. D., and C. D. Hundhausen. 2003. "An Experimental Study of the Effects of Representational Guidance on Collaborative Learning Processes." *Journal of the Learning Sciences* 12: 183–218.

Trotter, E., and C. Roberts. 2006. "Enhancing the Early Student Experience." *Higher Education Research and Development* 25: 371–386.

Van der Horst, H., and R. McDonald. 2004. *Outcomes-Based Education: Theory and Practice.* Centurion, South Africa: Tee Vee Printers and Publishers.

Van Offenbeek, M. 2001. "Processes and Outcomes of Team Learning." *European Journal of Work and Organizational Psychology* 10: 303–317.

Van Schalkwyk, G. J. 2007. "Choreographing Learning in Developmental Psychology Utilising Multigenerational Genograms and Reflective Journal Writing." *International Education Journal* 8: 127–138.

GERTINA J. VAN SCHALKWYK is an associate professor of psychology and head of the Department of Psychology, and former coordinator for professional development in the Centre for Teaching and Learning Enhancement at the University of Macau, China.

NEW DIRECTIONS FOR TEACHING AND LEARNING • DOI: 10.1002/tl

4

This chapter proposes supplementing traditional assessment strategies with innovative and authentic ways to evaluate students' performance on intended learning outcomes.

Authentic Assessment of Knowledge, Skills, and Attitudes

Brenda C. Litchfield, John V. Dempsey

Assessment! No one likes it, but everyone has to do it. It is a necessary part of teaching and learning and, for the most part, has not changed for hundreds of years. Teaching and learning have undergone reforms, improvements, programs, initiatives, and directions, yet the objective test has held its ground as the preferred assessment method in tertiary education around the world. In Asia, education in China, Hong Kong, Macao, Singapore, Japan, Taiwan, South Korea, and other countries is moving toward new practices in teaching and learning (Koh and Luke 2009). To be competitive in the global economy, these countries are finding that the centuries-old model of education with its emphasis on rote learning and objective testing is not adequately preparing their students. A new focus has been placed on creativity and problem solving. The introduction of general education course requirements in particular is based on developing students' knowledge, skills, and attitudes beyond the usual, narrowly focused curriculum of the past. This more comprehensive approach to teaching and learning necessitates new methods of assessment.

Even though researchers in higher education have proposed using authentic assessment to replace traditional assessment, these practices are slow to be implemented (Mueller 2011). Universities are routinely encountering more concern for accountability and specific directives from accrediting agencies, but things are still moving slowly, if at all. There are numerous reasons why many instructors in tertiary education have yet to implement authentic assessment: These include lack of knowledge of teaching methods and learning principles, general resistance to changing from the deeply embedded teaching practice of lecture, and the age-old comfort and reliance on objective testing. Adding to this is the opposition to the paradigm shift that is required. This paradigm shift takes the focus from the teacher as the central point in the classroom and moves it to the student (Fardows 2011).

New Directions for Teaching and Learning, no. 142, Summer 2015 © 2015 Wiley Periodicals, Inc.
Published online in Wiley Online Library (wileyonlinelibrary.com) • DOI: 10.1002/tl.20130

This dramatic shift is difficult for many instructors because to be effective it will require changes in both teaching and assessment.

This chapter is not advocating doing away with traditional assessment altogether. It certainly has its place in tertiary education. Testing to ascertain if students have acquired the knowledge base and basic skills is best done with traditional assessment because it is easy and fast. But traditional assessment should be only a part of the teaching and learning process. After students have acquired content knowledge, they must use it in a meaningful way. They must engage with the materials, the processes, and the essence of the subject. They must practice the skills that are performed by professionals in that field. They must practice and learn; problem solve and participate; revise and revisit. All this can be accomplished only through carefully constructed and relevant authentic assessments.

Asian Education

Education in Asian settings is widely acknowledged to be passive and non-interactive. This is based on the tradition and influence of Confucius. His students sat and listened to his every word and acquired knowledge in a one-way transmission of learning. This is in stark contrast to the Western model of education, where Socrates questioned and students answered, there was inquiry, and dialogue was encouraged and expected. Western students are expected to take responsibility for their own learning, be independent learners, and question their instructors. By contrast, Asian students consider their instructor to be authority figures who are to be respected, followed, and never questioned.

To make it easier when discussing this Confucian-based education, there is even an acronym, CHC, Confucian heritage culture (Biggs 1996). This applies generally to the cultures of Korea, Japan, China, Hong Kong, Taiwan, Malaysia, and Macao, and somewhat to Singapore. This method of teaching and learning is highly ingrained in students and instructors alike and has been the standard for thousands of years. This is not something that will be easily or quickly changed. As far back as 500 BC, tests were devised in China for civil servant job selection. Testing continues today in CHC contexts with several high-stakes tests determining the future of all students and their admission for limited positions in schools, universities, and government. This leads to considerable stress for them and their families. Students often spend weekends and holidays in special "cram schools" so they can pass the entrance exams, which are objective tests. So they study the way they are assessed: by memorizing material and reproducing it for the test.

Much has been written about Asian students and their ability and preference for memorizing material rather than learning at a deeper level. However, given their traditions in CHC contexts, students are simply doing what they have been taught and, moreover, *how* they have been taught. If instructors view students as preferring rote learning, then they often teach that way. Students, in turn, study in a way that is surface learning and memorize the facts that are presented in order to pass the tests. Instructors see this, and a self-fulfilling prophecy is realized (Kember 2000). It is only natural for students to adjust their learning strategies to match the assessment strategy.

Those who say Asian students actually prefer this type of teaching and learning and have difficulty learning any other way have not read the literature. Numerous studies have found that quite the opposite is true. When given a choice and asked about their preferences, the answers of Asian students are not significantly different from those of Western students (Biggs 1996, 2003; Kember 2000; Littlewood 2000, 2009; Tavakol and Dennick 2010). Asian students want to participate in activities, they welcome alternatives, and they do quite well when engaged in collaborative and outcomes-based forms of learning after they become comfortable with it. However, they are certainly products of their own culture when it comes to teaching and learning. This is a difficult barrier to surmount and will take quite some time to accomplish, but it can be done. It is impossible to change the entire learning culture and tradition of a country, but it may be possible to change teaching practices, which would help all students (Tavakol and Dennick 2010). This is where we begin. We change the teaching practices, which then lead to changes in assessment practices.

How Teaching Affects Assessment and Assessment Affects Teaching

The old saying is "If the only tool you have is a hammer, everything looks like a nail." If the only instructional strategy you know is lecture, then you think all students learn the same way. Lecturing assumes that all students learn the same: They cognitively process information the same way, at the same rate, with the same efficiency and same effectiveness. This, of course, is not true; in fact, it is impossible. We also know that students have different learning styles and areas of interest. A one-size-fits-all type of teaching is not effective for all students. Few students experience meaningful learning through lecture alone. Higher-level cognitive skills are not developed by passively listening to someone talk.

The most common assessment in tertiary education is still the objective test. This is because the most common method of teaching is still the lecture and information dissemination by the instructor (Reeves 2000). Certainly some would argue that there are wonderful, exciting lecturers out there, and it is true. And there are instructors who do add questions during the lecture. But whether the instructor is riveting or putting students to sleep, the lecture as an instructional strategy is dispensing bits and pieces of information at a rather low level of cognitive processing. Students are passively sitting and listening to the bits and pieces of content. These fragments of information, although strung together, rarely lend themselves to analysis, evaluation, or synthesis on the part of the students. If the delivery of information is in parts and fragments (even though well connected), the most common method of assessment is also in small pieces—the objective test. Essay questions can be created, but they are often a re-creation of what was "told" to students in the lecture. Students listen and then are tested on the material they have remembered just long enough for the test.

Lecturing and objective testing have a long partnership. Even in Western higher education, this combination is far too prevalent. If lecturing is the primary instructional strategy, delivering information at a low level of cognitive processing, then objective testing with its focus on memorization is the preferred way to test knowledge acquisition. If the test is objective, the instructor must present information in a way that will match the test—that is, via lecture. Each certainly drives the other. Deviation from either one is the first step toward authentic assessment. This will be a change for both instructors and students who are conditioned to the traditional assessment of objective testing.

For most university instructors, authentic assessment is a radical paradigm shift from teacher-centered to student-centered teaching and learning. Not having been trained in teaching methods, the majority of instructors continue to teach the way they were taught: via lecture and objective tests. Any one form of teaching or assessment is insufficient to adequately teach a subject or measure learning progress and student performance. Most university courses consist primarily of three components: lecture, traditional assessment, and assignments (see Figure 4.1). The majority of time in class is spent on lecture. Traditional assessment comprises a portion of the class sessions. Assignments lag behind and are often very few during a semester, given that the standard objective testing is so often used. In many courses there are only a midterm and a final exam.

A more effective model of university teaching and learning is based on five components shown in Figure 4.2. Each of the components is given equal time and importance. Lecture and traditional assessment are still parts of the course design but are now an equal portion of course activities rather than the majority of student experiences and instructor tasks.

Figure 4.1. Traditional Course Time Allocation

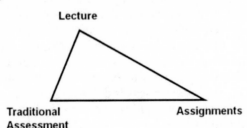

Figure 4.2. Ideal Course Time Allocation

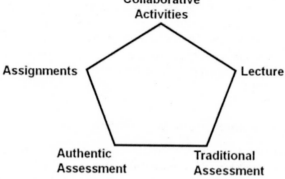

Assessment is an excellent source of feedback for students. Authentic assessment, in particular, is effective because it allows the instructor to provide positive feedback in a more motivational form than the usual numerical grade on a test (Litchfield, Mata, and Gray 2007). Through meaningful activities, students are able to determine where their weaknesses are and how to improve. Authentic assessment can also serve to increase student's self-regulated skills and develop intrinsic motivation for a course. Students working collaboratively can solve problems and develop meaningful modes of inquiry. They can simulate the real-world situations they will encounter in the workplace.

Assessment, however, is not only feedback for students. It is an integral part of teaching and learning that can help improve instructional materials, instructional strategies, teaching practices, and curriculum development. Instructors can use results to revise and improve all forms of classroom learning and practice. The key to using assessment to revise and improve teaching and learning is to select the right assessment. This is not objective assessment but rather *authentic* assessment. In authentic assessment, students learn the content and then apply it to meaningful and relevant tasks. Simply acquiring knowledge through memorization and lecture is not sufficient to demonstrate the essential skills necessary to be successful in a particular field or profession. What is the purpose of a college degree if the skills to perform in the real world have not been mastered? How often are people in a workplace given four distinct options to choose among when they are working in a group to solve a problem or create a product? Life is not a rigid, four-option, multiple-choice endeavor. Authentic assessment strongly emphasizes metacognition and processing of information, which is the key to learning (Azim and Khan 2012) and developing higher-order thinking skills (Koh, Tan, and Ng 2012).

Life consists of a myriad of options, problems, situations, and circumstances that require analysis, critical thinking, problem solving, and synthesis. These skills are developed through multiple interactions with others in collaborative activities. In order for students to be successful after they graduate, they must be prepared and guided through opportunities to develop these skills. Higher education programs should focus beyond simple acquisition and application of knowledge and skills (Vu and Dall'Alba 2008). Students must be active participants *in* and be responsible *for* their own learning. This is a drastic shift for students in Asian Confucian heritage cultures (Biggs 1996).

Student Expectations about Assessment

Student expectations in a course are tied to the assessment requirements (Meyers and Nulty 2009). While instructors consider assessment as a culminating course activity, students think about it at the beginning (Fardows 2011). The first course components most students are focused on are "What are the assignments, how many tests, and is there a final?" Students routinely scan this section of the syllabus first. They are not so much concerned with *what* they will learn but more with *how* it will be assessed. There is a different outlook in a course with objective testing than in a course with authentic assessments. Students match their learning strategies to what they expect will be required of them in terms of assessment (Biggs 2003), and this can vary from surface memorization to problem solving. For one course, flash cards are all that students need. In another course that requires complex knowledge structures and application of concepts and principles, flash cards are useless except perhaps for vocabulary words. Students adjust their plan of study, method of study, and time of study based on the assessments they will be required to complete in any given course.

The right kind of assessment can facilitate the right kind of learning. If we want students to develop critical thinking skills and higher-level knowledge that relate to their careers, we must provide them with the types of assessment that develop these skills. Students who are informed that the assessment for a course will be two multiple-choice tests and a multiple-choice final will study one way: they will memorize the material. This type of studying often produces surface learning at the expense of deep processing and integration of concepts and principles. Memorization can be done very effectively alone. Higher-level skills and the growth of critical thinking and problem-solving skills are best practiced with collaboration of others. It is the interaction that allows these skills to be developed. For classes with higher-level assessments, there is an increase in cognitive processing along with retention and transfer rather than a simple reproduction of material and isolated facts.

Students who have the opportunities to choose learning activities often choose activities that match the ways they prefer to learn. This type of assessment "takes into account variation in students' needs, interests and learning styles and attempts to integrate assessment and learning activities"

NEW DIRECTIONS FOR TEACHING AND LEARNING • DOI: 10.1002/tl

(Fook and Sidhu 2010, 153). Students who are creative may choose to do a video, design a game or a brochure about a topic, or produce a piece of art. More analytical students may write a comparison paper, critique a speech, or analyze an advertisement. Authentic assessment provides multiple opportunities for students to exhibit how they learn, and they usually participate more actively in their own learning.

When students view assessment practices as innovative and relevant, their perceptions regarding their tertiary studies can be significantly changed (Kearney and Perkins 2011). Students who see assessment as closely tied to relevant activities are more likely to engage in learning. This, in turn, can create a better appreciation and understanding of a subject area, thus developing a more intrinsic motivation about the course. Integrating relevance through meaningful collaborative activities and investigations can change students' perceptions about a course they may deem boring and tedious at the outset. Activities leading to assessments that require thought, involvement, and thinking are certainly innovative to many tertiary students because they have experienced objective testing for most of their educational careers. Assessments and their alignment with learning outcomes determine the activities instructors create and the activities students complete. This is not a quick and easy process for instructors or students to embark on—especially if they are not accustomed to collaborative teaching and learning in this manner.

Authentic Assessment

Definitions for the term "authentic assessment" abound and vary. Some use the terms "alternative," "authentic," and "performance assessment" interchangeably. Others are specific that "authentic" is different from "alternative" and "performance." For the purposes of this chapter, "alternative assessment" is defined as a form of assessment where students engage in real-world activities where they can realistically apply knowledge and skills with fidelity. Authentic assessments are when students perform a task rather than select answers, as in objective testing. These tasks are related to the topic they are studying, as in general education courses. In upper-level courses, authentic assessment relates closely to career goals and practices. Students can participate more fully in activities and real-world experiences that have a direct bearing on their careers, thus preparing them for challenges that lie ahead. According to Gulikers, Bastiaens, and Kirschner (2004, 69), authentic assessment is "an assessment requiring students to use the same competencies, or combinations of knowledge, skills, and attitudes that they need to apply in the criterion situation in professional life." Students should be involved in situations and simulations that give them a deeper understanding of the demands that they will experience in their careers.

The quality of work in authentic assessment is judged on preset criteria that are given to students and fully explained in detail. The use of a definitive set of criteria is beneficial to both instructors and students. It serves as a concrete guide for students, which can help alleviate confusion and foster confidence (Keller 2010) because they know what is expected of them. Instructors can also use criteria lists as grading sheets. This makes grading easier and more precise. In addition, the use of rubrics can provide guidance and specificity for students to follow.

Authentic assessment is different in every way from traditional assessment. The practices of traditional assessment revolve around the infamous, long-practiced, overused multiple-choice test, where students usually memorize content and choose the correct answer. This form of assessment offers students little in the way of real-world or application experiences they can add to their knowledge, skills, and attitude base in a subject area. Merely memorizing content long enough for a test does not foster deep learning and does not lead to higher-level thinking.

Yet objective testing continues to be the predominant form of assessment in Asia and as well as in many other cultures. Although it is well known that traditional assessment does not provide students with realistic assessment of learning, why is it still used? It is easy to construct and fast to grade; it ranks students quickly and is just what the name implies—traditional. Old habits die hard. Authentic assessments take time at both the creation and the grading stages. Few university instructors are trained in how to create any type of assessments, especially not authentic ones (Reeves 2000). They lack the knowledge to construct and use authentic assessments and therefore continue to use the traditional assessments, often as the sole method for evaluating student learning and progress.

Authentic assessment has not been widely implemented in tertiary education in most subject areas. Some areas, however, have long used authentic assessment. Teachers spend time in classrooms, nurses and physicians spend time in hospitals, and counselors complete internships, to name a few. Even in vocational training, car mechanics work on cars, welders weld, and carpenters build. No one would dream of letting students in any of these professions graduate without practice and internships. But what about so many other areas? Quite a few professions are now moving toward more client-based, patient-based, or skill-based curricula. These types of learning cannot be demonstrated through traditional objective assessment methods. They involve a complex set of skills that are difficult, if not impossible, to assess through paper-and-pencil tests. In order to demonstrate these complex skills in their careers, students must engage in them prior to graduation. This requires a different type of assessment strategy.

Herrington and Herrington (2006) created authentic assessment guidelines divided into four groups: (1) context, (2) student factors, (3) task factors, and (4) indicators. These four areas should form the framework for developing assessment to maximize student achievement and proficiency in a subject area. Authentic assessments must be grounded in real-world contexts. This means they should provide students with experiences that are relevant to the subject area and closely mimic situations and practices they will encounter in their careers and everyday work experiences. Spending years in college without actually practicing the essential skills that will be applied in the workplace is unacceptable. The degree to which students experience the fidelity of authentic experiences is a result of the quality of activities provided by course requirements, classroom activities, and assessment.

The most important consideration in the student factors category is that students engage in activities and assignments where they can use critical thinking and problem-solving skills. This cannot be accomplished in the traditional classroom when lecture is the primary mode of instruction. Students need to interact with other students in working relationships where they can produce a product that reflects what they have learned and can be applied in the real world. It is through this interaction that they practice decision making, negotiation, and simulate what they will do on the job or in situations where they must interact successfully with other individuals.

Task factors comprise a wide range of options where students use a variety of methods to achieve their learning goal. Students may be writing, interviewing, observing, creating artistic products, analyzing, and using a numerous skills and strategies to complete the activity. All students do not learn the same way, so they should not all be assessed the same way. The range of task factors can be extensive but still related to the same learning outcomes of the course. The closer the task factors match student learning styles, the more involved students will be in the project or product. Students working collaboratively can divide the tasks so each student's assignment more closely matches interests and abilities.

Benefits of Authentic Assessment.   Why spend the time and effort creating authentic assessments for students? Knowledge is constructed when people interact with the world and their surroundings (Vu and Dall'Alba 2008). Students may learn to memorize in isolation, but the application of that knowledge requires further synthesis at a higher level to be meaningful and relevant. The use of authentic assessment produces more in-depth learning and transfer (Fook and Sidhu 2010; Kearney and Perkins 2011; Svinicki 2004). When students participate in authentic tasks, they become actively involved in their learning. They are no longer passive recipients of information delivered by the instructor. More of the responsibility of learning is shifted *to* students *from* the instructor. They become part of the process and, in turn, become empowered. Completing relevant activities and investigations is a more valid indicator of their attainment of knowledge, skills, and attitudes. These three important aspects of learning are combined when students apply what they have learned to real-world activities and especially when they work collaboratively.

Students engaging in authentic assessments develop meaningful modes of inquiry, which can lead to increased critical thinking and problem solving. Carefully constructed activities can guide students to research, evaluate, and synthesize information in order to produce a product that will exhibit what they have learned. These products can be multifaceted and demonstrate learning and progress in ways traditional assessment cannot. Authentic assessment activities address the components of Keller's (2010) ARCS Model components: *attention, relevance, confidence,* and *satisfaction.*

Attention is gained through innovative activities and authentic assignments that are created for students. Students tend to become involved in activities that get their attention. Another characteristic of attention is that it must not only be gained but maintained. This is done through variability and change of pace. Both of these can be accomplished in the classroom through interesting activities and group collaboration.

Personal choice and meaningful activities help develop *relevance.* When students see the value in an assignment, they expend more time on task and energy. Time on task usually leads to increased competence. Activities that provide leadership and interactive activities build relevance because students are performing roles and are involved in activities relevant to them. Collaborative learning activities factor strongly into helping students see the relevance in a course by giving them numerous opportunities for social interaction.

Giving students specific criteria for assignments facilitates *confidence.* Each activity in an authentic assessment must include detailed instructions and guidelines, thus ensuring that students are not confused by the procedures and requirements for completion. Students develop more confidence in a subject or course when they can choose among alternatives. Confidence is essential in both choosing a learning activity and the way in which learning is exhibited. Students could choose to report on a particular topic by giving an oral report, writing a paper, creating a model or poster, or even filming a video. Being able to choose a method that more closely relates to student interest and ability builds confidence. Rubrics are also helpful for building confidence because they delineate the specifics of the levels of accomplishment and establish instructor expectations.

Satisfaction is realized through the application of real-world situations and circumstances where students apply what they have learned. Rather than choosing an answer on a test, they are producing product that has meaning and is a concrete indication of their learning progress. Only by getting involved with the material, making judgments, and synthesizing content can students integrate their knowledge, skills, and attitudes. Role-plays and simulations afford authentic activities that provide students with a vast array of authentic experiences related to future career situations.

An additional benefit of authentic assessments is that students learn to develop self-regulated skills. Students who use self-regulated skills perform better academically than unregulated students and are most likely to achieve higher academic goals (Pintrich and DeGroot 1990; Zimmerman and Martinez-Pons 1986). Self-regulation (Zimmerman 2000) involves setting goals, monitoring performance, evaluating performance, and revising efforts based on perceived learning progress. When students are engaged in activities requiring them to choose, plan, keep track of their progress, and think about their accomplishments, they are using self-regulated learning skills. This important set of skills cannot be adequately developed when the instructor is the sole director in the educational process. In a teacher-centered environment, students are passive recipients of learning. In student-centered classrooms, students are more responsible for their own learning, thus developing self-regulated and metacognitive skills.

Research has shown that students who are self-regulated tend to be more motivated, engaged, active, and involved in their learning. This, in turn, makes them more likely to seek help when they need it (Arbreton 1998; Karabeck 2002, 2003). Authentic assessments, by design, afford more engagement and active learning. Students are immersed in the creation of an artifact that demonstrates what they have learned in a much more relevant way than traditional assessment. By providing authentic assessment activities, an instructor can offer students opportunities not only to learn more but also to develop additional skills essential to succeeding in a learning environment. All this, of course, is dependent on the quality of the assessment and the skill of the instructor in conveying its relevance and criteria for successful completion.

Creating Authentic Assessments.   Meyers and Nulty (2009, 567) suggest five curriculum design principles that should guide the development of teaching and learning materials along with tasks and experiences. Course activities should do five things:

1. Be authentic, real-world, and relevant.
2. Be constructive, sequential, and interlinked.
3. Require students to use and engage with progressively higher-order cognitive processes.
4. Be aligned with each other and the desired learning outcome.
5. Provide challenge, interest, and motivation to learn.

A course designed with these principles in mind can provide students with numerous learning experiences that afford knowledge acquisition that can lead to authentic practice. The five principles cannot be achieved in courses where lecture and objective testing are the primary course activities. It takes knowledge of teaching and learning theories, along with innovative practices, to create a course that encompasses this wide range of principles that will ensure students develop the metacognitive skills to participate in their own learning.

As Cumming and Maxwell (1999) point out, there are first-order and second-order expectations of a task. First-order expectation is the development of knowledge and skills necessary to accomplish the task. This is the usual knowledge acquisition that is practiced in all classrooms: facts, figures, concepts, principles, and "information" of the subject that is easily assessed by objective testing. This part of learning can be delivered by the instructor or read by students. Many universities are now putting lectures online for students to watch and review before they come to class. Students can watch them numerous times if they need to. So the production and delivery of the "information" of a subject is something all instructors know how to do.

The second-order expectation, however, is not something many instructors do at all, much less, do well. Instruction and learning often stop with the first-order expectation. The second-order expectation is the immersion in the activity and performance of actual behaviors relevant to the situation and subject area. This is where real learning occurs. This is where application, evaluation, and synthesis are practiced and perfected. Therefore, to accomplish effective second-order expectations, authentic tasks must be realistic, engaging, and carefully aligned with higher-level learning outcomes. Objective testing cannot assess these authentic tasks. Students cannot be solely lectured to and then be expected to complete activities that require critical thinking and problem solving. Interim steps would include instructor guidance along with collaborative interactions to practice and display the skills and attitudes necessary to succeed in the second-order expectation task.

To create more effective and authentic assessments that address second-order expectations, assignments must be well thought out and carefully designed. When assignments are more intellectually challenging, students are more likely to create work products that are of higher quality (Koh and Luke 2009). Of prime importance in authentic assessment is the fidelity of assignments to actual situations that illustrate and enhance the content area and prepare students for future careers and problems of practice. Assessments must be constructed to give students the opportunity to play an active role in their own learning. Effective alternative assessments must be integrated throughout a course beginning with learning outcomes. Innovative classroom activities, relevant assignments, and student participation in learning are essential. Effective assessment is not something that can be tacked on to the end of days or weeks of classroom lecture (Burton 2011). Assignments must be relevant to course material and student interests in a way that is seamless and integrated with the learning outcomes of the course. Ensuring that assignments are relevant requires that learning outcomes represent a range of cognitive levels focusing on the higher-level ones.

Grading Authentic Assessments with Rubrics.   The use of portfolio assessment and of scoring rubrics for performance assessments are both considered best practices in the collaborative teaching and learning classroom (Frey, Schmitt, and Allen 2012). Portfolios are excellent indicators of student progress and can be created more easily with the use of rubrics as guides for students. Although not widely used in tertiary education, rubrics have been in use for many years and have helped instructors and students by making performance requirements clearer and more specific. Students and instructors both see benefits from the use of rubrics (Gaytan and McEwan 2007). From a student point of view, rubrics help define the learning goals and expectations of the instructor. No longer do students have to guess what the instructor is looking for in an assignment. The delineation of levels of competency provided by rubrics can instill additional confidence in students. For instructors, rubric use streamlines the grading process and makes it more impartial.

In a study investigating perceptions of rubric use, Andrade and Du (2005) found that the use of rubrics was considered to do the following: (1) communicate teacher expectations, (2) facilitate student planning, (3) facilitate revision, (4) facilitate reflection, (5) result in equitable grading, (6) improve quality of work, and (7) lower anxiety. Each of these seven reasons points out the benefit of using rubrics as a basis for grading. For authentic assessments, rubrics are essential. The nature of authentic assessments is such that they cannot be evaluated objectively. There are levels of proficiency that must be specified and illustrated in order to fully inform students of what is expected of them to be successful in the activity or product production. Rubrics can also be used for student self-assessment and self-reflection (Palloff and Pratt 2009). This can further the development of self-regulated skills, which are essential to the development of students as effective learners.

Conclusion

For students to be successful in their careers, they must practice the knowledge, skills, and attitudes that are directly related to what they will encounter in the workplace. Instructors in tertiary education must pay closer attention to this need and develop course content and authentic assessment that are relevant and prepare students. Such preparation cannot be accomplished with traditional assessment and objective testing. There must be a shift from teacher-centered to student-centered and collaborative teaching and learning where students learn not only content but also how to apply it in meaningful ways. The progression must go beyond the first-order expectations (content, facts, information) to the second-order expectations (active involvement, construction, performing).

Asian students learn and study the way they do because, like all students, they adjust their study methods to match assessment methods. If the predominant method of instruction is lecturing, the predominant method of study is memorization for objective testing. In many classrooms, there are few assignments and a heavy reliance on one or two extensive tests. Students engage in the long-practiced cramming for tests and rarely interact with course materials in any higher-order cognitive levels.

This change in teaching and assessment will not be easy or swift. It requires a different mind-set and preparation on the part of faculty that is

NEW DIRECTIONS FOR TEACHING AND LEARNING • DOI: 10.1002/tl

supported by the administration. Faculty development must be provided in a manner that models the kinds of skills and attitudes of authentic assessment. It must be ongoing and systematic as well as systemic. It is not necessary to do away with traditional assessment altogether. It still has a necessary function in tertiary education. But it must become an equal part of classroom practices that is shared with collaborative learning, lecture, meaningful assignments, and authentic assessment. As a sole determiner of student progress evaluation, objective testing is an insufficient method of assessment.

Authentic assessment has been shown to increase student learning, involvement, time on task, motivation, and self-regulated learning skills. It provides students with meaningful activities that relate directly to real-world situations and that prepare them to function successfully when they leave the university. It is the responsibility of all instructors to provide their students with the best education possible. This means giving them the practice to experience and develop the knowledge, skills, and attitudes they need to succeed in their careers and in life. This can best be accomplished through authentic assessment that is carefully crafted as an integral part of every course a student takes.

References

Andrade, H., and Y. Du. 2005. "Student Perspectives on Rubric-Referenced Assessment. Practical Assessment." *Research and Evaluation* 10. http://pareonline.net/getvn.asp?v=10&n=3.

Arbreton, A. 1998. "Student Goal Orientation and Help-Seeking Strategy Use." In *Strategic Help Seeking: Implications for Learning and Teaching*, edited by S. A. Karabeck, 95–116. Mahwah, NJ: Lawrence Erlbaum.

Azim, S., and M. Khan. 2012. "Authentic Assessment: An Instructional Tool to Enhance Students' Learning." *Academic Research International* 2: 314–320.

Biggs, J. B. 1996. "Western Misperceptions of the Confucian-Heritage Learning Culture." In *The Chinese Learner: Cultural, Psychological, and Contextual Influences*, edited by D. A. Watkins and J. B. Biggs, 45–67. Hong Kong, China: CERC and ACER.

Biggs, J. B. 2003. *Teaching for Quality Learning at University*, 2nd ed. Maidenhead, UK: Open University Press.

Burton, K. 2011. "A Framework for Determining the Authenticity of Assessment Tasks: Applied to an Example in Law." *Journal of Learning Design* 4: 20–28.

Cumming, J. J., and G. S. Maxwell. 1999. "Contextualizing Authentic Assessment." *Assessment in Education* 6 (1): 77–194.

Fardows, N. 2011. "Investigating Effects of Evaluation and Assessment on Student Learning Outcomes at the Undergraduate Level." *European Journal of Social Sciences* 23: 34–40.

Fook, C., and G. Sidhu. 2010. "Authentic Assessment and Pedagogical Strategies in Higher Education." *Journal of Social Sciences* 6: 153–161.

Frey, B. B., V. L. Schmitt, and J. P. Allen. 2012. "Defining Authentic Classroom Assessment." *Practical Assessment, Research & Evaluation* 17. http://pareonline.net/pdf/v17n2.pdf.

Gaytan, J., and B. C. McEwan. 2007. "Effective Online and Instructional Assessment Strategies." *American Journal of Distance Education* 21: 117–132.

Gulikers, J., T. Bastiaens, and P. Kirschner. 2004. "The Five-Dimensional Framework for Authentic Assessment." *Educational Technology Research and Development* 52: 67–85.

Herrington, J., and A. Herrington. 2006. "Authentic Conditions for Authentic Assessment: Aligning Task and Assessment." In *Proceedings of the 2006 Annual International Conference of the Higher Education Research and Development Society of Australasia Inc (HERDSA): Critical Visions: Thinking, Learning and Researching in Higher Education: Research and Development in Higher Education*, Vol. 29, edited by A. Bunker and I. Vardi, 141–151. Milperra, NSW: HERDSA.

Karabeck, S. A. 2002, July. "Effects of Subjective Classroom Context on College Students' Help Seeking." Paper presented at the International Congress of Applied Psychology, Singapore.

Karabeck, S. A. 2003. "Help Seeking in Large College Classes: A Person-Centered Approach." *Contemporary Educational Psychology* 28: 37–58.

Kearney, S. P., and T. Perkins. 2011, October. "Improving Engagement: The Use of 'Authentic Self and Peer Assessment for Learning' to Enhance the Student Learning Experience." Paper presented at the Academic and Business Research Institute Conference, Las Vegas, Nevada.

Keller, J. M. 2010. *Motivational Design for Learning and Performance*. New York, NY: Springer.

Kember, D. 2000. "Misconceptions about the Learning Approaches, Motivation, and Study Practices of Asian Students." *Higher Education* 40: 99–121.

Koh, K., and A. Luke. 2009. "Authentic and Conventional Assessment in Singapore Schools: An Empirical Study of Teacher Assignments and Student Work." *Assessment in Education: Principles, Policy and Practice* 16: 291–318.

Koh, K. H., C. Tan, and P. T. Ng. 2012. "Creating Thinking Schools through Authentic Assessment: The Case in Singapore." *Educational Assessment, Evaluation and Accountability* 24: 135–149.

Litchfield, B., J. Mata, and L. Gray. 2007. "Engaging General Biology Students with Learning Contracts." *Journal of College Science Teaching* 37: 34–39.

Littlewood, W. 2000. "Do Asian Students Really Want to Sit and Obey?" *ETL Journal* 54: 31–36.

Littlewood, W. 2009. "Chinese Learners and Interactive Learning." In *Internationalizing the University: The Chinese Context*, edited by T. Coverdale-Jones and P. Rastall, 206–222. London, England: Palgrave Macmillan.

Meyers, N., and D. Nulty. 2009. "How to Use (Five) Curriculum Design Principles to Align Authentic Learning Environments, Assessment, Students' Approaches to Thinking and Learning Outcomes." *Assessment and Evaluation in Higher Education* 34: 565–577.

Mueller, J. 2011. *The Authentic Toolbox*. http://jfmueller.faculty.noctrl.edu/toolbox/howdoyoudoit.htm.

Palloff, R. M., and K. Pratt. 2009. *Assessing the Online Learner*. San Francisco, CA: Jossey-Bass.

Pintrich, P. R., and E. V. DeGroot. 1990. "Motivated and Self-Regulated Learning Components of Classroom Academic Performance." *Journal of Educational Psychology* 82: 33–40.

Reeves, T. C. 2000. "Alternative Assessment Approaches for Online Learning Environments in Higher Education." *Journal of Educating Computing Research* 23: 101–111.

Svinicki, M. 2004. *Learning and Motivation in the Postsecondary Classroom*. San Francisco, CA: Jossey-Bass.

Tavakol, M., and R. Dennick. 2010. "Are Asian International Medical Students Just Rote Learners?" *Advances in Heath Science Education* 15: 369–377.

Vu, T. T., and G. Dall'Alba. 2008, December. "Exploring an Authentic Approach to Assessment for Enhancing Student Learning." Paper presented at the annual meeting of the Australian Association for Research in Education Brisbane, Australia.

Zimmerman, B. J. 2000. "Attaining Self-Regulation: A Social-Cognitive Perspective." In *Handbook of Self-Regulation: Theory, Research, and Applications*, edited by M. Boekaerts, P. R. Pintrich, and M. Zeidner, 13–39. San Diego, CA: Academic Press.

Zimmerman, B., and M. Martinez-Pons. 1986. "Development of a Structured Interview for Assessing Student Use of Self-Regulated Learning Strategies." *American Educational Research Journal* 23: 614–628.

BRENDA C. LITCHFIELD *is a professor of instructional design and development at the University of South Alabama.*

JOHN V. DEMPSEY *is the director of the Innovation in Learning Center at the University of South Alabama.*

This chapter explores the ways in which a relational understanding of the education process and the use of collaborative technologies in the connectivist tradition might inform and transform university teaching.

Connectivism and the Use of Technology/Media in Collaborative Teaching and Learning

Neena Thota

The importance of collaboration between learners, as a way of improving learning outcomes and motivating greater engagement with learning (Dillenbourg 1999; Johnson and Johnson 1994), is a recurrent theme in all the chapters of this book. Collaborative learning with technology embraces the use of digital, mobile, and networked devices within a group of learners. The growth of Internet usage and the availability of a wide variety of Web-based tools present the twenty-first-century learner and teacher with new ways to deal with knowledge and skills development. The rise of the technologically savvy "digital native" (Prensky 2001) presents new challenges for teachers accustomed to traditional lecturing.

In computer-supported collaborative learning (CSCL), the focus is on learning through collaboration with other students via social interaction mediated by computer environments (Stahl, Koschmann, and Suthers 2006). It is a form of networked learning that promotes interactions between learners, between learners and tutors, and between a learning community and its learning resources (Goodyear et al. 2004). Networked learning supports the integration of electronic media with face-to-face teaching and learning, emphasizes collaborative learning, and promotes cooperative knowledge production as well as individual and independent learning (Roberts 2004). Computer-supported learning environments mediate the collaborative processes of shared conceptions that include interaction, discussion, argumentation, and reflection (Kirschner, Paas, and Kirschner 2009; Roschelle and Teasley 1994). Socially oriented software, such as wikis, blogs, collaborative documents, social networks, and learning

NEW DIRECTIONS FOR TEACHING AND LEARNING, no. 142, Summer 2015 © 2015 Wiley Periodicals, Inc.
Published online in Wiley Online Library (wileyonlinelibrary.com) • DOI: 10.1002/tl.20131

management systems, enable learner collaboration and act as enablers of twenty-first-century teaching (Churches 2008).

Outcomes-based collaborative teaching and learning (CTL) with technologies provides a powerful antidote to the Confucian way of learning through memorization and teaching by imparting information. The emphasis on student-centered learning and the shift from a focus on information delivery to communication, from passive learning to inquiry-based and interactive engagement, and from individual learners to socially situated and real-world contexts (Conole 2007; Shelly, Gunter, and Gunter 2010) make collaborative technologies an ideal medium for encouraging critical thinking among Asian learners. In recent years, connectivism (Downes 2005; Siemens 2004) has been advanced as a learning theory for the digital age.

This chapter presents connectivism, with its emphasis on interaction for knowledge development, as the foundation for designing courses for Asian learners at university level. It gives some examples of courses using technology for collaborative learning, presents connectivism as a suitable theory for learning in the digital age, and highlights issues and concerns resulting from using collaborative media and connectivism for teaching and learning. Next, the chapter presents an example of a master's course integrating technological media for collaborative learning among multicultural learners and concludes with a reflection on using connectivism and technology/media in CTL.

Theoretical Basis for Teaching and Learning with Technology

There are many advocates for a theoretical approach to integrate technological media in the learning context. Elkind (2004) argues that a philosophical basis for use of technology gives the impetus required for encouraging alignment of teacher, curricular, and societal readiness. Theoretical approaches to the use of technology-enhanced learning are related to learning theories and result in instructional designs that range from formal instruction to authentic contexts for learning (Mayes and de Freitas 2007). A list of the key features of some of these learning theories (Mayes and de Freitas 2004) follows.

- *Associative learning theory*, which refers to building concepts or competencies through activities, led to instructional design theories (Gagne 1977; Merrill and Twitchell 1994) that focus on presentational and testing capabilities of technology.
- *Cognitivist learning theory*, with its emphasis on mental models and metacognitive processes, resulted in tutoring software (Anderson et al. 1995) that projected the expert view.
- *Situative learning theory*, which refers to developing practice in a particular community (Lave and Wenger 1991), is marked by the use of collaborative technologies (McConnell 2000).

NEW DIRECTIONS FOR TEACHING AND LEARNING • DOI: 10.1002/tl

Constructivist learning theory has also influenced the use of technologies for learning. Constructivist-based technologies serve as cognitive learning mind tools to scaffold, engage, and facilitate knowledge construction and reflective thinking (Jonassen 2000). Constructivist learning, deriving from the work of Piaget (1978), influenced instructional design that enables the construction of active knowledge through programming, simulation, and modeling technologies (Papert 1980). Social constructionism (Vygotsky 1978) focuses on the importance of discussion in communicative technologies (Scardamalia and Bereiter 1994, 2006).

From a phenomenographic learning theory perspective, educational media serves to mediate between the world and the learner (Laurillard 2002). Information technology is considered as offering the potential to open up new patterns of variation (Marton and Trigwell 2000) to make new kinds of learning possible and to make students aware of the diversity of perspectives. Technologies are employed so that students experience critical aspects of variation in the object of learning and in order to present a range of opportunities for a higher level of learner engagement by offering new ways of representing knowledge.

Approaches to course design with technology can thus draw from a gamut of theories of learning. Three well-known theoretically based models for learning with technologies include Mayes and Fowler's (1999) conceptualization cycle, Salmon's (2003) five-stage model, and Laurillard's (2002) conversational framework, which are described next.

Conceptualization Cycle. Mayes and Fowler's (1999) conceptualization cycle blends instructivist approaches that emphasize content presentation with constructivist approaches and include aspects of face-to-face teaching to engage the learner in the active performance of tasks. Iterative cycles characterize conceptualization, where the learner interacts with new information, constructs new or refined concepts through application and testing, and dialogues with tutors and peers to create and test new concepts. Mayes and Fowler emphasize task-based learning and dialogue to enhance learning.

Five-Stage Model. Unlike Mayes and Fowler's (1999) model, which highlights interaction and dialogue, Salmon's (2003) five-stage model for computer-mediated communication focuses on scaffolding individual development and is the outcome of Salmon's action research project with online networking. Salmon acknowledges the influence of personal construct theory (Kelly 1955) and social constructionism (Vygotsky 1978) in her work. The model emphasizes access and motivation for students to use online systems, online socialization, information exchange, knowledge construction, and development of affective values.

Conversational Framework. Laurillard (2002, 2009), whose work is particularly influential in higher education institutions in the United Kingdom, designed the conversational framework based on the characterization of teaching and learning as an iterative conversation (Kolb 1984;

Pask 1976; Vygotsky 1978). Laurillard adopts the phenomenographic view of variation in ways of knowing and the relational view of contextual influences on student learning approaches. The instructional design process, as envisioned by Laurillard (2009), combines the pedagogies of constructionism and social learning to provide collaborative learning interactions. The practicalities of mediating to support all aspects of the learning process emerge through a classification of educational media as narrative, interactive, communicative, adaptive, productive, and collaborative.

Collaborative Technologies

Knowledge Forum (Scardamalia and Bereiter 2006) is an example of an online collaborative environment that provides features for collaborative problem solving. Built on the original work with the computer-supported intentional learning environment (CSILE; Scardamalia and Bereiter 1994), the forum focuses on constructivist knowledge-building pedagogy. Scardamalia and Bereiter see students not as passive learners or as inquirers but as active participants in the process of advancing knowledge and developing knowledge-building competencies. Students can create and share views using multimedia and can contribute theories, models, or reference material. The forum provides tools for scaffolding, feedback, and revision and keeps track of advances in group knowledge.

One example of CSILE, in the Asian context, was the course for teacher participants in Hong Kong (Chan 2001). This course integrated computer-supported collaborative learning with regular teaching in a graduate course in educational psychology. The participants produced online learning notes reflecting their understanding of the course readings and discussions. The findings showed that exposure to other participants' conceptions and perceptions deepened the nature of the reflections, especially for those participants who engaged in collaborative note construction. The study found that contrary to the representation that Chinese students do not disagree with each other, the students in this course queried and challenged each other's ideas and made advances to the discourse.

Cloudworks, a social networking site (Conole, Galley, and Culver 2011), is another example of theory-based use of collaborative tools. At this site, community spaces called cloudscapes act like multi-user blogs and discussion forums. The site has been developed to enable social and participatory practices such as peer critiquing, sharing, user-generated content, aggregation, and personalization among learners. Cloudworks derives its theoretical basis from four frameworks:

1. communities of inquiry that include cognitive, teaching, and social presence (Garrison, Anderson, and Archer 2000);
2. communities of practice that view learning as social participation (Wenger 1998);

3. activity theory that emphasizes context in mediating learning (Engeström 1987); and
4. actor-network theory that underscores interaction between nodes made up of human and nonhuman actors (Latour 1997).

The preceding review and examples show that instructors can draw on a vast body of research on learning theories to design ways to enhance learning supported by technology and in particular for CTL. However, Siemens (2004) argues that behaviorist, cognitivist, and constructivist learning theories do not address learning that resides in technology-driven networks of information or learning that happens within social and business organizations. Together with Downes (2006), he proposes connectivism as a learning theory for the digital age.

Connectivism. Connectivism integrates principles from chaos, network, and complexity and self-organization theories, underpinned by the epistemology of connective knowledge, pedagogy, and theories of innovations in technology (Siemens 2004). It is rooted in the understanding (Downes 2005, 2006; Siemens 2006) that:

1. knowledge is emergent, distributed across information networks, and resides in multiple individuals;
2. the acquisition of knowledge rests in the interactions and the diversity of views and opinions within networked communities of learning and personal networks;
3. technology frees learners from the cognitive operations of information storage and retrieval, keeps learners current in a rapidly evolving information ecology, and enables learners to see the interconnections in differing fields of knowledge;
4. socialization is evidence of connectedness and the learner is empowered to learn and reflect through conversation and interaction and through the creation and sharing of meaningful digital artifacts, such as blogs, Twitter posts, and multimedia Webcasts; and
5. informal and lifelong learning are significant parts of the learning experience that includes work-related tasks.

Connectivist learning environments are seen as:

- open to all perspectives;
- encouraging diversity of viewpoints;
- allowing individual autonomy to learners to contribute according to their own knowledge, values, and decisions; and
- furthering interactive knowledge production.

E-learning 2.0 empowers students to think and act through conversation, interaction, sharing, creation, and participation (Downes 2006). The idea of a personal learning environment in which a learner can interact with a network of people, services, and resources from home or workplace and engage in learning driven by personal interest or through informal or formal program requirements is also introduced.

Four types of activities drive learning in a connectivist environment: (1) aggregation of resources; (2) relation of new knowledge to old; (3) creation of artifacts to show learning; and (4) sharing of insights with other learners (Kop 2011). The connectivist learner is seen as nurturing and maintaining connections to facilitate continual learning and as developing the ability to synthesize and recognize connections among fields, ideas, and concepts. The abilities to find and evaluate current, accurate, and up-to-date knowledge and to make decisions about what to learn as part of the learning process are seen as critical outcomes.

A Connectivist Course.   The "Places to Go: Connectivism & Connective Knowledge" course by George Siemens and Stephen Downes at the University of Manitoba (Downes 2008) was the first course explicitly underpinned by the principles of connectivism. It is referred to as a massive open online course (MOOC) due to the large number of student enrollments in subsequent years. In the course, a wiki acted as the base for links to online videos, audios, and documents. Videoconference sessions (Elluminate, Skype) were held with experts and broadcasted (UStream). The Moodle learning management systems was used for online discussions. Email, RSS, and an aggregator (gRSShopper that was developed by Downes) gathered student posts for distribution. Communication was maintained through a mailing list offered by Google Groups and through Twitter messages. The open structure of the course based on connectivist principles led students to manage their learning by setting up their own learning communities in Google groups, Facebook, and Second Life. Students were inspired to create resources using concept maps, network diagrams, images, and Wordle diagrams.

The course is a testimony to the connectivist principles of autonomy, diversity, openness, and connectedness/interactivity with users developing their own personal learning networks and using new media in innovative ways (Mackness, Mak, and Williams 2010; Mak, Williams, and Mackness 2010). The course design emphasizes that institutions are not the sole providers of course material and that social networks, online media, and free software have led to emergent models of learning (Downes 2008).

Issues with Collaborative Technologies.   The pedagogical challenges to the use of collaborative technologies (Laurillard 2009) are the identification of the theoretical underpinnings and dealing with the technological evidence or artifacts that facilitate the interactions between learner and teacher and between learners. Hindrances for teachers (Reeves, Herrington, and Oliver 2004) also include misapplication of tools, lack of development time and funds, institutional regulations, unreliability of technology infrastructure, and the need to develop new professional and technological competencies to deal with learner support and anxieties. Students' continued effort and engagement with the collaborative activity and shared knowledge cannot be guaranteed but is crucial for the outcomes (Roschelle and Teasley 1994). Limiting social interaction only to computer-supported cognitive processes undermines the value of social interaction for group dynamics and group learning (Kreijns, Kirschner, and Jochems 2003).

Cross-cultural interactions are often known to be problematic in group work. The collectivism versus individualism dimension and the long-term versus short-term dimension identified in cultural situations supposedly influence collaborative learning (Hofstede 1980; Hofstede and Bond 1988). The notion of face saving in collectivist societies with short-term orientations could affect online discussions and collaborative project work. Vatrapu and Suthers (2007) suggest that cultural differences may result in (1) the adoption by East Asian learners of a more holistic approach to referencing concept maps and groups, whereas Western learners look for evidence of relations between individual objects; and (2) East Asian learners being more likely to give higher ratings to their peers for collaborative work as compared to Western learners who tend to measure for individual competencies. Several studies have identified problems in cross-cultural interactions in learning with technologies in diverse areas, such as user interface design, usability evaluation, interaction with World Wide Web, information systems, computer-supported cooperative work, and online learning (Vatrapu and Suthers 2007).

Issues with Connectivism.   Connectivism is not without its share of critics. The chief concern seems to be whether connectivism warrants being accorded the status of a new learning theory similar to social constructionism and constructivism, which explain learning in social communities (Kerr 2007; Kop and Hill 2008; Verhagen 2006). Another concern is that in an unstructured connectivist space for learning, the direction of learning is influenced by "network leaders" who shape emergent knowledge, while learners who are not self-directed or who do not possess high levels of creative and innovative thinking are often left confused by the goals of the course and the amount of information available (Anderson and Dron 2011; Kop 2011). Autonomy to learn can be interpreted by some participants as lack of support, while openness can lead to some participants disengaging from connecting and sharing (Mackness, Mak, and Williams 2010).

While acknowledging that connectivism is an influential theory in networked learning, Bell (2010) argues for widening the knowledge base for experiential reports of connectivist learning and teaching. Bell further contends that connectivism can be justified only if it is related to the scope and purposes of the learning context, is supported by the experience and philosophical stances of the researchers/practitioners, and is funded by grants for research/evaluation. Siemens (2006) himself acknowledges that time, budget, technological infrastructure, competencies of staff and students, and institutional readiness impact on success of implementing a connectivist approach. It is clear that further research is needed to create engaging learning activities that maximize the potential of emergent and innovative technologies.

Course Design with Collaborative Technologies

As with any collaborative learning task, incorporating collaborative technologies in the classroom requires planning and preparation. Siemens (2006, 41) suggests an approach for course design that includes six items:

1. definition of the intended learning outcomes;
2. deliberation on the nature of the learning tasks;
3. matching each task with the appropriate technological medium;
4. consideration of the profile and needs of learners;
5. incorporation of metalearning elements; and
6. provision of diverse tools/spaces/ecologies.

Next I describe a course design based on the connectivist view of learning with technologies. The intended learning outcomes are clearly defined, the learning tasks are matched with appropriate technological media, and provision is made for students to use multiple tools and learning spaces to present their projects. The course design demonstrates how the instructor addresses the learning needs of the students and the disparity in the technological skills and competencies.

Course Context and Learning Outcomes.   The Education and Technology course (MEd112) at the University of Saint Joseph, Macao, is taken by students working toward a degree in Master's in Education. The four-week course (June 2011) had fourteen students. The multicultural group was composed of twelve teachers from schools (kindergarten, primary, and secondary) and from universities in Macao. The remaining two students, though not working as teachers, aspired to take up the teaching profession eventually.

The MEd112 course was geared toward providing an understanding of learning theories (behaviorist, cognitive, constructivist, and connectivist) and models for teaching with technology. The primary focus in the course was on the use of technology for learning and teaching, online learning activities, technology-driven lesson development, using tools for literature review and qualitative and quantitative data analysis, and presentation of projects using digital media formats. The students were expected to explore technology for teaching and research in education and to collaborate and share digital resources. They were also expected to develop an understanding of the social, ethical, human, and legal issues involved in the use of technology and to be aware of the historical development and future directions in technology.

Table 5.1. Alignment of Learning Outcomes and Assessment Activities with Technology and Tools in MEd112

Intended Learning Outcome/Assessment	Task Nature	Related Technology/ Tools
Review and evaluate Web 2.0 tools/learning objects, and present your findings to your peers.	Pair work	Presentation in class using digital media
Design a lesson plan incorporating the use of educational technology for a course you teach.	Individual work	Lesson plan using media
Explain in a lesson plan your choice of different pedagogic models for using technology in education.		Electronic document for lesson plan
Discuss with your peers your views on the potential role and effectiveness of technology in education.	Group work	Online discussion forum
Collaborate with your team to harvest, apply, and share digital media in teaching and learning.	Group work	Shared digital repository
Reflect on the collaborative work that you have undertaken with your peers in this course.	Individual work	Electronic journal

The intended learning outcomes, on which students were assessed for the course, were constructively aligned with an appropriate assessment task (Biggs 1996). The outcomes denoted integrative and extended understandings from Bloom's Digital Taxonomy (Churches 2008) that recognizes the collaborative interactions and processes necessitated by the introduction of information and communication technologies into classrooms. Table 5.1 shows the learning outcomes aligned with specific assessment tasks related to the course. Each of the assessment tasks varied in nature (individual/ pair/group work) and was mapped to a related technology/tool to elicit the required learning outcome(s).

The assessments were graded holistically using the structure of the observed learning outcome (SOLO) levels that differentiate between qualitative levels of learning (Biggs and Collis 1982). Additionally, the next outcomes, based on the taxonomy of the affective domain (Krathwohl, Bloom, and Masia 1964), were integrated within all the assessment criteria to account for the relation and sharing components of the course design:

- *Work productively.* Value and consistently show a strong work ethic, cooperation, and initiative while working in pairs/groups.

- *Communicate ideas effectively.* Communicate in written and oral presentations, both formally and informally, and offer constructive critiques of the presentations of others.
- *Demonstrate* ability for organization and internalization of values.
- *Reflect on and manage* one's own learning and development as a responsible learner.
- *Discuss* a wide variety of useful personal initiatives indicative of a growing commitment to lifelong learning.
- *Demonstrate* consistency in the set of values, and show development of a worldview and a philosophy of life (be an active learner; participate in class activities; be self-motivated).

Table 5.2 shows the teaching and learning activities in the MEd112 that were mapped to a related technology/tool. Effort was made to avoid proprietary software and to introduce students to open source/free alternatives.

Connectivist Principles.   The course was designed with the four connectivist principles in mind: aggregation, relation, creation, and sharing. The next sections explain how the tools were used for learning and teaching in the MEd112 course to enable access to information and resources (aggregation), to relate new knowledge to earlier developed knowledge through

Table 5.2. Alignment of Teaching and Learning Activities with Technology/Tools in MEd112

Teaching/Learning Activities	Technology/Tools
Introduce the module and assignments	Moodle (learning management system)
Introduce general field of study	Web links to resources
Introduce digital media for teaching and learning	Online multimedia reusable learning objects
Assess expertise and motivation of learners; gather feedback about course	Online questionnaires within Moodle
Search and summarize information	WebQuest, Mindmaps (electronic), web 2.0 tools
Share experience and new knowledge	Blogs, bookmarking sites, wikis, social networking sites, RSS feeds, podcasting, virtual worlds
Conduct self- and peer evaluation	Online journal within Moodle; online forum at blogger.com
Conduct a literature review and research writing	Open source referencing software
Discuss social, ethical, human, security, and legal issues	Guidelines and open source software
Create digital artifacts	Electronic lesson plan with demonstration of learning and testing media

reflection on resources and experience (relation), to create digital artifacts to show new learning (creation), and to share digital artifacts with the community of learners (sharing).

Aggregation.   The course material was available to the students via Moodle (the university-specified learning management system), which connected students, course material, and lecturer in a structured manner. Information about learning theories and pedagogic models for learning with technology was provided through links to e-books, e-journals, online videos, and Web pages that stored archived knowledge. Similarly, information about open source/free reference managers, qualitative data analysis packages, statistical analysis software, and utility programs (antivirus, password management, and file sync) was made available for students to explore and choose.

Relation.   The students used the electronic journal in Moodle for their reflective writing and for self- and peer evaluation. Feedback was given to the students for all assignments. On the first day of the course, students were directed to a questionnaire in the course page designed to elicit details of their technological skill levels and to gauge their motivation and self-efficacy levels. Feedback from the questionnaire enabled the instructor to tailor the course for a wide spectrum of skill levels and enabled the identification of and just-in-time intervention for students who were apprehensive about their competencies with technologies.

Creation.   Students were required to present their theoretically grounded lesson plans using media of their choice. The lesson plan tested new ideas and approaches using technologies. The students used Blogger, WebQuest, and Second Life to present their lesson plans. They integrated digital tools such as Flickr, Sketchcast, YouTube, podcasts, animations, visualizations, e-books, electronic flash cards, and learning objects to achieve their teaching and learning outcomes.

Sharing.   During the course, the students enrolled in a shared space at blogger.com. The online forum facilitated self-expression, debate, and dialogue. A shared database was set up in Moodle for students to provide links to their lesson plans. Some groups set up a Facebook page to communicate and share resources within their group. Other students used Google docs to share documents. Links to new knowledge and information sourced from personal networks were shared through bookmarking sites, such as Delicious and Diigo, and by subscribing to RSS feeds.

Reflection on MEd112.   Teaching a connectivist-based course opened up a new vision of teaching with technology. Learning to negotiate new technologies and media along with the students led to new insights into how challenging the process can be. The students learned as much from each other as they did from the instructor and were able to choose supporting pedagogies for their lesson plans, deploy digital tools, and use taxonomies for defining their outcomes and assessments. The course evaluation questionnaire, the journal entries, and the informal discussions with students revealed some issues with student learning. According to Siemens (2006), the learning path in a connectivist environment increases in complexity as learners negotiate the phases of connectivist learning. The different phases provided their own set of difficulties for students in the MEd112 course. These phases are discussed next.

Awareness and Receptivity. In this stage, learners acquire the skills for navigating information and scaffold the provision of resources and tools. The small class size in the MEd112 course allowed the instructor to give individual help to students to acquire basic skills in accessing information. The provision of extensive help resources in Moodle served to frame the learning to some extent. However, it was difficult for nonnative English speakers to grasp and navigate the enormous amount of information and to relate to the learning theories and models that were at their disposal.

Connection Forming. In this stage, learners began to form a personal network, develop skills for selecting and filtering information, and engage in affective and emotive roles in decision making. Developing these skills and taking decisions about what to use proved harder for some students in the MEd112 course than for others. Some students tended to constantly check with the instructor to determine whether they were choosing the "right" tool or media. For these students, taking ownership of their learning proved to be the biggest challenge in the course.

Contribution and Involvement. In this stage, learners begin to actively contribute resources, artifacts, and ideas, leading to shared understandings or collaborative knowledge creation. All the students in the MEd112 course were able to contribute and the application of the suggested digital media was often related to their own teaching context. The adoption of tools sourced by others was more prominent at the end of course, as students had by then gained an understanding of the tools through the presentations and discussions.

Pattern Recognition. In this stage, learners were capable of recognizing emerging patterns and trends related to information and knowledge creation. The lesson plans presented by the students in the MEd112 course were evidence of their capabilities to relate information and knowledge creation to their own teaching contexts. There was a pleasing congruence of learning outcomes, teaching activities, and tools and media. Some students reported showing their lessons using technology to their colleagues. In one case, the school administrator asked the master's student to hold a workshop for other teachers to learn how to design a course with learning technologies.

Meaning Making. In this stage, learners made sense of emerging patterns and shifting trends and recognized how to negotiate multiple viewpoints, perspectives, and opinions. It was obvious that the non-Asian students in the MEd112 course initially dominated discussions. In the beginning, the Asian students mostly concurred with the opinions expressed, but as the course progressed, it was interesting to see their increased contribution and the expression of their forceful opinions.

Praxis.   In this stage, learners engaged in metacognition, active reflection, and critical evaluation and transformation of the personal learning network. All participants in the MEd112 course experienced learner anxiety in terms of unfamiliarity with digital tools. However, their journal entries also testified to an increased level of critical reflection on their own learning and that of others. In particular, the shift from fear of using new technologies to increased confidence and even enjoyment was clearly visible toward the end of the course.

The MEd112 course was designed with connectivist principles in mind. Although not as massive as other online courses based on connectivist ideas, the MEd112 course managed in some measure to make autonomy, diversity, openness, and connectedness/interactivity a reality for the Asian participants. While encouraging independent learning, autonomy was delimited by instructor-provided resources and the requirements of the assignments. Diversity of learning and teaching styles for the novice teachers was supported within the bounds of learning theories and pedagogic frameworks. Free expression of thoughts and ideas was urged, though it took some time for some participants to be comfortable with discussing and debating in an open forum. Connections made within a group were strong and fruitful for group learning and even with other groups within the class. However, connections to worldwide networks were not visible. Overall, MEd112 offered a unique opportunity to observe how applying connectivist principles enriched everyone's learning.

Conclusion

This chapter described the learning theories that guide practitioners in using technologies for CTL. Connectivism is a theoretical lens to encourage self-directed and collaborative learning among Asian learners in higher education settings. An example of a connectivist-based master's course with a description of the outcomes and learning activities provided a guide, demonstrating that the definition of outcomes and the creation of learning activities with technological tools are complex procedures that do lead to collaborative, creative, and innovative means of learning. The chapter also highlighted the issues that instructors and learners face in using technology, particularly in connectivist learning environments.

References

Anderson, John R., Albert T. Corbett, Kenneth R. Koedinger, and Ray Pelletier. 1995. "Cognitive Tutors: Lessons Learned." *Journal of the Learning Sciences* 4: 167–207.

Anderson, Terry, and Jon Dron. 2011. "Three Generations of Distance Education Pedagogy." *International Review of Research in Open and Distance Learning* 12: 80–97.

Bell, Frances. 2010. "Connectivism: Its Place in Theory-Informed Research and Innovation in Technology-Enabled Learning." *International Review of Research in Open and Distance Learning* 12: 98–118.

Biggs, John B. 1996. "Enhancing Teaching through Constructive Alignment." *Higher Education* 32: 347–364.

Biggs, John B., and Kevin F. Collis. 1982. *Evaluating the Quality of Learning: The SOLO Taxonomy.* New York, NY: Academic Press.

Chan, Carol K. K. 2001. "Promoting Learning and Understanding through Constructivist Approaches for Chinese Learners." In *Teaching the Chinese Learner: Psychological and Pedagogical Perspectives,* edited by David A. Watkins and John B. Biggs, 181–203. Hong Kong, China: University of Hong Kong.

Churches, Andrew. 2008. "Bloom's Digital Taxonomy." Edorigami Wikispaces. http:// edorigami.wikispaces.com/file/view/bloom%27s+Digital+taxonomy+v3.01.pdf.

Conole, Gráinne. 2007. "Describing Learning Activities." In *Rethinking Pedagogy for a Digital Age: Designing and Delivering E-Learning,* edited by Helen Beetham and Rhona Sharpe, 81–91. New York, NY: Routledge.

Conole, Gráinne, Rebecca Galley, and Juliette Culver. 2011. "Frameworks for Understanding the Nature of Interactions, Networking, and Community in a Social Networking Site for Academic Practice." *International Review of Research in Open and Distance Learning* 12 (3): 119–138.

Dillenbourg, Pierre. 1999. "What Do You Mean by 'Collaborative Learning'?" In *Collaborative Learning: Cognitive and Computational Approaches,* edited by Pierre Dillenbourg, 1–19. Oxford, UK: Elsevier.

Downes, Stephen. 2005. "An Introduction to Connective Knowledge." http://www .downes.ca/post/33034.

Downes, Stephen. 2006. "Learning Networks and Connective Knowledge." http://it.coe .uga.edu/itforum/paper92/paper92.html.

Downes, Stephen. 2008. "Places to Go: Connectivism & Connective Knowledge." *Innovate Online* 5 (1). Accessed March 26, 2011. http://www.innovateonline.info/pdf /vol5_issue1/Places_to_Go-__Connectivism_&_Connective_Knowledge.pdf.

Elkind, David. 2004. "The Problem with Constructivism." *Educational Forum* 68: 306–312.

Engeström, Yrjö. 1987. *Learning by Expanding. An Activity-Theoretical Approach to Developmental Research.* Helsinki, Finland: Orienta-Konsultit.

Gagne, Robert M. 1977. *The Conditions of Learning and Theory of Instruction,* 3rd ed. New York, NY: Holt, Rinehart and Winston.

Garrison, D. Randy, Terry Anderson, and Walter Archer. 2000. "Critical Inquiry in a Text-Based Environment: Computer Conferencing in Higher Education." *Internet and Higher Education* 2: 87–105.

Goodyear, Peter, Sheena Banks, Vivien Hodgson, and David McConnell. 2004. "Research On Networked Learning: An Overview." In *Computer-Supported Collaborative Learning Book Series Volume 4: Advances in Research on Networked Learning,* edited by P. Dillenbourg, 1–10. Dordrecht, the Netherlands: Kluwer Academic.

Hofstede, Geert. 1980. *Culture's Consequences: International Differences in Work-Related Values.* Beverly Hills, CA: Sage.

Hofstede, Geert, and Michael Harris Bond. 1988. "The Confucius Connection: From Cultural Roots to Economic Growth." *Organizational Dynamics* 16: 5–21.

Johnson, David Walcott, and Roger T. Johnson. 1994. *Learning Together and Alone: Cooperative, Competitive, and Individualistic Learning,* 5th ed. Boston, MA: Allyn and Bacon.

Jonassen, David H. 2000. *Computers as Mindtools for Schools: Engaging Critical Thinking,* 2nd ed. Upper Saddle River, NJ: Merrill.

Kelly, George A. 1955. *The Psychology of Personal Constructs.* New York, NY: Norton.

Kerr, Bill. 2007. "A Challenge to Connectivism." *learningEvolves Wikispaces.* http:// learningevolves.wikispaces.com/kerr.

Kirschner, Femke, Fred Paas, and Paul Kirschner. 2009. "A Cognitive-Load Approach to Collaborative Learning: United Brains for Complex Tasks." *Educational Psychology Review* 21: 31–42.

Kolb, David. 1984. *Experiential Learning: Experience as the Source of Learning and Development*. Englewood Cliffs, NJ: Prentice Hall.

Kop, Rita. 2011. "The Challenges to Connectivist Learning on Open Online Networks: Learning Experiences during a Massive Open Online Course." *International Review of Research in Open and Distance Learning* 12: 19–38.

Kop, Rita, and Adrian Hill. 2008. "Connectivism: Learning Theory of the Future or Vestige of the Past?" *International Review of Research in Open and Distance Learning* 9: 1–13.

Krathwohl, David R., Benjamin S. Bloom, and Bertram B. Masia. 1964. *Taxonomy of Educational Objectives: The Classification of Educational Goals. Handbook II: Affective Domain*. New York, NY: David McKay.

Kreijns, Karel, Paul A. Kirschner, and Wim Jochems. 2003. "Identifying the Pitfalls for Social Interaction in Computer-Supported Collaborative Learning Environments: A Review of the Research." *Computers in Human Behavior* 19: 335–353.

Latour, Bruno. 1997. "On Actor-Network Theory: A Few Clarifications (Working Paper)." http://www.bruno-latour.fr/sites/default/files/P-67%20ACTOR-NETWORK.pdf.

Laurillard, Diana. 2002. *Rethinking University Teaching: A Conversational Framework for the Effective Use of Educational Technology*, 2nd ed. London, UK: RoutledgeFalmer.

Laurillard, Diana. 2009. "The Pedagogical Challenges to Collaborative Technologies." *International Journal of Computer-Supported Collaborative Learning* 4: 5–20.

Lave, Jean, and Etienne Wenger. 1991. *Situated Learning: Legitimate Peripheral Participation*. Cambridge, UK: Cambridge University Press.

Mackness, Jenny, S. F. John Mak, and Roy Williams. 2010. "The Ideals and Reality of Participating in a MOOC." In *Proceedings of the Seventh International Conference on Networked Learning*, edited by L. Dirckinck-Holmfeld, V. Hodgson, C. Jones, M. de Laat, D. McConnell, and T. Ryberg, 266–274. Lancaster, England: Lancaster University.

Mak, S. F. John, Roy Williams, and Jenny Mackness. 2010. "Blogs and Forums as Communication and Learning Tools in a MOOC." In *Proceedings of the Seventh International Conference on Networked Learning*, edited by L. Dirckinck-Holmfeld, V. Hodgson, C. Jones, M. de Laat, D. McConnell, and T. Ryberg, 275–284. Lancaster, England: Lancaster University.

Marton, Ference, and Keith Trigwell. 2000. "Variatio Est Mater Studiorum." *Higher Education Research & Development* 19: 381–395.

Mayes, Terry, and Sara de Freitas. 2004. "Stage 2: Review of E-Learning Theories, Frameworks and Models." *Jisc E-Learning Models Desk Study* 1. www.csus.edu/indiv/s/stonerm/Mayes-DeFreitas--E-LearningModels-CompLaurillardPPT.pdf.

Mayes, Terry, and Sara de Freitas. 2007. "Technology Enhanced Learning: The Role of Theory." In *Rethinking Pedagogy for a Digital Age*, edited by Helen Beetham and Rhona Sharpe, 17–30. New York, NY: Routledge.

Mayes, Terry, and Chris Fowler. 1999. "Learning Technology and Usability: A Framework for Understanding Courseware." *Interacting with Computers* 11: 485–497.

McConnell, David. 2000. *Implementing Computer Supported Cooperative Learning*, 2nd ed. London, UK: Kogan Page.

Merrill, David M., and David Twitchell. 1994. *Instructional Design Theory*. Englewood Cliffs, NJ: Educational Technology.

Papert, Seymour. 1980. *Mindstorms: Children, Computers, and Powerful Ideas*. New York, NY: Basic Books.

Pask, Gordon. 1976. "Styles and Strategies of Learning." *British Journal of Educational Psychology* 46: 128–148.

Piaget, Jean. 1978. *The Development of Thought: Equilibrium of Cognitive Structures*, translated by A. Rosin. New York, NY: Viking Press.

Prensky, Marc. 2001. "Digital Natives, Digital Immigrants Part 1." *On the Horizon* 9: 1–6.

Reeves, Thomas, Jan Herrington, and Ron Oliver. 2004. "A Development Research Agenda for Online Collaborative Learning." *Educational Technology Research and Development* 52: 53–65.

Roberts, Gillian. 2004. "Teaching Using the Web: Conceptions and Approaches from a Phenomenographic Perspective." In *Advances in Research on Networked Learning*, edited by P. Goodyear, S. Banks, V. Hodgson, and D. McConnell, 221–244. Dordrecht, the Netherlands: Kluwer Academic.

Roschelle, Jeremy, and Stephanie D. Teasley. 1994. "The Construction of Shared Knowledge in Collaborative Problem Solving." In *Computer-Supported Collaborative Knowledge*, edited by C. O'Malley, 69–97. Heidelberg, Germany: Springer-Verlag.

Salmon, Gilly. 2003. *E-Moderating: The Key to Teaching and Learning Online*, 2nd ed. London, UK: Taylor and Francis.

Scardamalia, Marlene, and Carl Bereiter. 1994. "Computer Support for Knowledge-Building Communities." *Journal of the Learning Sciences* 3: 265–283.

Scardamalia, Marlene, and Carl Bereiter. 2006. "Knowledge Building: Theory, Pedagogy, and Technology." In *Cambridge Handbook of the Learning Sciences*, edited by K. Sawyer, 97–118. New York, NY: Cambridge University Press.

Shelly, Gary B., Glenda A. Gunter, and Randolph E. Gunter. 2010. *Teachers Discovering Computers: Integrating Technology and Digital Media in the Classroom*, 6th ed. Boston, MA: Cengage Learning.

Siemens, George. 2004. "Connectivism: A Learning Theory for the Digital Age." *International Journal of Instructional Technology and Distance Learning* 2: 3–10.

Siemens, George. 2006. *Knowing Knowledge*. Vancouver, BC, Canada: Lulu Press.

Stahl, Gerry, Timothy Koschmann, and Dan Suthers. 2006. "Computer-Supported Collaborative Learning: An Historical Perspective." In *Cambridge Handbook of the Learning Sciences*, edited by K. Sawyer, 409–426. Cambridge, UK: Cambridge University Press.

Vatrapu, Ravi, and Dan Suthers. 2007. "Culture and Computers: A Review of the Concept of Culture and Implications for Intercultural Collaborative Online Learning." In *Lecture Notes in Computer Science*, edited by Toru Ishida, Susan Fussell, and Piek Vossen, 260–275. Berlin, Germany: Springer.

Verhagen, Plon. 2006. "Connectivism: A New Learning Theory." Accessed November 10, 2011. http://elearning.surf.nl/e-learning/english/3793.

Vygotsky, Lev S. 1978. *Mind in Society: The Development of Higher Psychological Functions*, 2nd ed., edited by Mary Gauvain and Michael Cole. Cambridge, MA: Harvard University Press.

Wenger, Etienne. 1998. *Communities of Practice: Learning, Meaning, and Identity*. Cambridge, UK: Cambridge University Press.

NEENA THOTA *is the program coordinator for information systems in the faculty of creative industries at the University of Saint Joseph, Macao SAR, China.*

INDEX

The premise of inclusive teaching works to demonstrate that all people can and do learn. Educators and administrators can incorporate the techniques of inclusive learning and help learners retain more information.
ISBN 978-11190-36470

TL139 **Multidisciplinary Collaboration: Research and Relationships**
Karen Weller Swanson, Editor
The Scholarship of Teaching and Learning (SoTL) has been a movement in higher education for many years. This volume of *New Directions for Teaching and Learning* focuses on this scholarship and how collaborations among and between disciplines can strengthen education and the ways in which students are taught. The community of scholars that exists at any institution can provide a fertile ground for interdisciplinary collaboration that can enliven the educational process and the research that supports it. The chapters within this volume are written by individuals from many different disciplines who teach and who use SoTL to inform their own practice and as a method to share what they have done with others.
ISBN 978-11189-80569

TL138 **Hidden Roads: Nonnative English-Speaking International Professors in the Classroom**
Katherine Grace Hendrix, Aparna Hebbani, Editors
This issue uses the powerful narrative of autoethnography to make visible the existence of international professors and teaching assistants who speak English as a Second Language. These important, but often invisible, individuals contribute daily to the education of students within the US postsecondary educational system. Much of the research on international faculty in the classroom has focused on gathering voices of US students as the subjects, so there is a notable absence in the literature of voices of the nonnative English speaker in the classroom. This volume adds to the literature by covering a variety of experiences, such as faculty of color teaching intercultural communication, international teaching assistants' attitudes toward their US students, and the challenges to existing cultural assumptions in the US classroom. These experiences—in the form of challenges and contributions—are foregrounded and highlighted in their own right.
ISBN 978-11189-23092

TL137 **Active Learning Spaces**
Paul Baepler, D. Christopher Brooks, J. D. Walker, Editors
When we think about some of the main concepts that are embodied in the recent teaching and learning paradigm shift, we think about student engagement, active learning, collaboration, and peer instruction. And when we reflect upon the impediments to making these things happen in courses, instructors often indict the physical spaces in which they teach. The configuration of classrooms, the technology within them, and the behaviors they encourage are frequently represented as a barrier to enacting student—centered teaching methods, because traditionally designed rooms typically lack flexibility in seating arrangement, are configured to privilege a speaker at the front of the room, and lack technology to facilitate student collaboration. But many colleges and universities are redesigning the spaces in which students learn, collapsing traditional lecture halls and labs to create

new, hybrid spaces—large technology-enriched studios—with the flexibility to support active and collaborative learning in larger class sizes. With this change, our classrooms are coming to embody the 21st-century pedagogy which many educators accept, and research and teaching practice are beginning to help us to understand the educational implications of thoughtfully engineered classrooms—in particular, that space and how we use it affects what, how, and how much students learn.
ISBN 978-11188-70112

TL136   ***Doing the Scholarship of Teaching and Learning: Measuring Systematic Changes to Teaching and Improvements in Learning***
Regan A. R. Gurung, Janie H. Wilson, Editors
The Scholarship of Teaching and Learning (SoTL) should be an integral part of every academic's life, representing not only the pinnacle of effortful teaching, but also standing side by side with more conventional disciplinary scholarship. Although practiced by many instructors for years, SoTL has garnered national attention resulting in a spate of new journals to publish pedagogical research. SoTL helps students, fosters faculty development, and has been integrated into higher education in *Scholarship of Teaching and Learning Reconsidered* (Hutchings, Huber, & Ciccone, 2011). This volume provides readers with challenges that will motivate them to engage in SoTL and take their pedagogical research further. We include many key features aimed to help both the teacher new to research and SoTL and also researchers who may have a long list of scholarly publications in non-pedagogical areas and who have not conducted research.
ISBN 978-11188-38679

TL135   ***From Entitlement to Engagement: Affirming Millennial Students' Egos in the Higher Education Classroom***
Dave S. Knowlton, Kevin Jack Hagopian, Editors
This volume of New Directions for Teaching and Learning addresses theories and practices surrounding the entitled, self-absorbed students called Millennials. Stereotypical Millennials are often addicted to gadgets, demand service more than education, and hold narrow perspectives about themselves and those around them; when seen through this lens, Millennial students can understandably frustrate the most dedicated of professors.

   The contributors to this volume show how new and better educational outcomes can emerge if professors reconsider Millennials. First and foremost, many of these students simply don't fit their stereotype. Beyond that, the authors urge faculty to question commonly held assumptions, showing them how to reevaluate their pedagogical practices, relationships with students, and the norms of college classrooms. Contributors focus on practical means to achieve new and more evocative outcomes by treating Millennial students as serious collaborators in the learning process, thereby helping those students to more closely identify with their own education. The assignments that professors give, the treatment of topics that they broach, and the digital tools that they ask students to employ can shift students' concerns away from a narrow focus on impersonal, technical mastery of content and toward seeing themselves as Millennial thinkers who fuse their lives with their learning.
ISBN 978-11187-70108

NEW DIRECTIONS FOR TEACHING AND LEARNING
ORDER FORM SUBSCRIPTION AND SINGLE ISSUES

DISCOUNTED BACK ISSUES:

Use this form to receive 20% off all back issues of *New Directions for Teaching and Learning*.
All single issues priced at **$23.20** (normally $29.00)

TITLE	ISSUE NO.	ISBN

Call 1-800-835-6770 or see mailing instructions below. When calling, mention the promotional code JBNND to receive your discount. For a complete list of issues, please visit www.josseybass.com/go/ndtl

SUBSCRIPTIONS: (1 YEAR, 4 ISSUES)

☐ New Order   ☐ Renewal

U.S.	☐ Individual: $89	☐ Institutional: $335
Canada/Mexico	☐ Individual: $89	☐ Institutional: $375
All Others	☐ Individual: $113	☐ Institutional: $409

Call 1-800-835-6770 or see mailing and pricing instructions below.
Online subscriptions are available at www.onlinelibrary.wiley.com

ORDER TOTALS:

Issue / Subscription Amount: $ _____

Shipping Amount: $ _____
(for single issues only – subscription prices include shipping)

Total Amount: $ _____

SHIPPING CHARGES:	
First Item	$6.00
Each Add'l Item	$2.00

(No sales tax for U.S. subscriptions. Canadian residents, add GST for subscription orders. Individual rate subscriptions must be paid by personal check or credit card. Individual rate subscriptions may not be resold as library copies.)

BILLING & SHIPPING INFORMATION:

☐ **PAYMENT ENCLOSED:** *(U.S. check or money order only. All payments must be in U.S. dollars.)*

☐ **CREDIT CARD:** ☐ VISA ☐ MC ☐ AMEX

Card number _____Exp. Date_____

Card Holder Name_____Card Issue # _____

Signature _____Day Phone_____

☐ **BILL ME:** *(U.S. institutional orders only. Purchase order required.)*

Purchase order # _____
Federal Tax ID 13559302 • GST 89102-8052

Name_____

Address_____

Phone_____ E-mail_____

Copy or detach page and send to: **John Wiley & Sons, One Montgomery Street, Suite 1000, San Francisco, CA 94104-4594**

Order Form can also be faxed to: **888-481-2665**

PROMO JBNND